My
Habitat for Humanity

The *(Mostly)* Good Old Days

David Johnson Rowe

ISBN 978-1-257-90671-0

Dedication

*"Two are better than one ... for if one falls down,
the friend can help the other up."*
(Ecclesiastes 4:9-10)

To Paul Davis and Julie Peeples,
two of the best parts of the 'good old days.'
They walked the talk,
and lived out St. Paul's mandate to
"weep with those who weep,
and rejoice with those who rejoice"
as Habitat's Chaplains for all those near and far.

To Frank and Janet Stoffle,
who truly had the courage of their convictions.

Contents

Acknowledgments — vi

1   Memoirs and Memories: *Caveat Emptor*   p. 1

2   My Habitat World   p. 4

3   Millard Fuller and Me   p. 17

4   The Elephant in the Room   p. 30

5   Americus, Georgia   p. 52

6   Africa   p. 68

7   Nicaragua   p. 90

8   India   p. 100

9   The U.S. of A.   p. 115

10   The End   p. 128

FOCI, Habitat and me   p. 136

Acknowledgments

My life with Habitat was only possible because of two very understanding church congregations, who allowed me great freedom:

The Church in the Gardens, Forest Hills, New York City
and
The First Baptist Church of Melrose, Massachusetts.

Special thanks to the great people at the First Baptist Church of Pittsfield, Massachusetts, who ended my forced exile in the wilderness, hired me as damaged goods, and nursed me back to health.

Good people stood with me through the good old days, great people got me through the really bad days, from immediate family to far-flung friends.

My Greenfield Hill Congregational Church family showed me the path to forgiveness by living it.

Alida Ward brought this book to life with editing that would have made her Aunt Betsy proud.

And once again, deepest gratitude to David Moss for the inspired cover design and for the back cover.

May God bless you all, even as I have been blessed by you.

Chapter One

Memoirs and Memories: Caveat Emptor

Fired.

For a lot of years that was my singular memory of a long life with Habitat for Humanity. Fired for confronting my friend, Millard Fuller, over his sexual behavior. Fired, according to Millard, for being a defender of women. Fired for doing what I was hired to do. Fired for believing that Habitat and Millard and all of us could be better than we were. Fired for being naïve and sometimes just plain stupid. That's my story.

This particular slice of my life covers my years with Habitat for Humanity (HFH), from 1977 to 1991. These were years of dynamism, creativity, and energy beyond anything I had ever experienced or imagined. I saw a glorious world of mission; I met spiritual giants who roamed the world cognito and incognito; I saw Christians and churches rise above the pettiness of their divisions in order to attempt bold things for God.

Glorious mission, spiritual giants, bold things for God. I chose those phrases quite intentionally. I want you to wonder if I am exaggerating. I am not. I got to see mission at its best, church at its best, and people at their best.

But there was heartache, too. It took me twenty years to be able to remember that those were "Good Old Days" worth remembering, worth telling others about, worth being grateful for. Now that I am remembering I can wish I had done it earlier. But I'm not one of those spiritual giants. What I am is a Habitat veteran, more notorious than famous. That's where the 'caveat emptor' comes in. *Buyer beware.*

I was President of Habitat For Humanity, International, for nine years, on the Board for thirteen, before joining the staff as Director of Operations. This gave me a front row seat for the explosive growth of Habitat from almost its first days into the heady years of great growth and popularity.

It is also true that I was on the committee to investigate Habitat's founder, Millard Fuller. Several women complained of sexual harassment by Millard, which we found to be completely truthful. Somehow or other that got me fired, leaving a bad taste in my mouth that took twenty years to cleanse, for which I blame only myself.

If it is true that time heals all wounds, or at least grants some perspective, I am ready to tell my Habitat story. It is a story well worth writing; I can only hope that it is well worth reading. It is worth writing because the writing of it forced me to remember the good old days. And they were good. I was with Habitat in one way or another for fourteen years, plus two additional years that I was on severance pay after being fired, still living a few blocks from Habitat headquarters.

From the day I was fired until the day I began a new pastoral ministry was exactly two years, seven hundred and thirty days. Those were the only lousy days, and even some of them were pretty good. Yet the bitterness of those lousy days, the brokenness and betrayal among friends, the preference for injustice among a few, clouded my eyes for a very long time. I even had standing instructions that Habitat was not to be mentioned in my obituary when I died. If Jesus could have his "missing years" from age twelve to thirty, I figured I could have my missing years from 1977 to 1993. Ignore it. Don't mention it. Pretend it never happened. Wish it never happened.

Slowly, excruciatingly slowly, the cloud lifted and I allowed myself to remember. Mostly I remember stories and feelings. I am not settling scores, so there aren't many names included in this book. The good guys know who they are. And the bad guys? Well, I put myself as number one, so why list others? Whatever went wrong in the years 1977 to 1991, whatever failures or weaknesses or oversights happened, they all happened on my watch. I had a front row seat for all of it; I had power and influence and position. Sometimes all of that did some good ... sometimes it didn't.

I recognize that even the phrase "the good old days" is subjective. I seem to be suggesting that there was a certain time in the past when Habitat was clearer, purer, innocent, and idealistic. But for someone starting out with HFH today, their involvement will be *their* good old days, some day.

So this isn't meant to be a commentary on today's HFH, or tomorrow's, or yours. This is my story, a little window into some pretty extraordinary times.

Of course, I run the risk of being in a long line of "old fogies" who "wax nostalgic" about "the good old days." But what the heck. I do that about baseball, movies, rock n' roll, even about pizza. It seems to be part of the package of growing older, to assume that the good old days were better.

So let me be clear. Number one, I am not saying that my good old days were better. HFH is surely better today. But number two, coming from me, with my shady and controversial history with Habitat and with Millard Fuller, it may be helpful to hear me acknowledge that there were good old days worth remembering! And some great lessons for life and faith along the way.

Welcome to my Habitat world.

Chapter Two
My Habitat World

Part 1

In 1975 I went to Africa for the first time. Motivated by a devastating famine in Sub Saharan Africa and the bruising apartheid of South Africa, I joined a team from my denomination to see the challenges, opportunities and ministries of Africa first hand.

I saw need that I had never imagined. I met spiritual giants who changed the course of my life and ministry with their combination of energy, creativity, dynamism, and faith.

By the time I returned to my church in upstate New York I was one of the world's leading experts on Africa, world mission and famine. I say that only somewhat tongue-in-cheek. This was the mid-seventies, before the Internet and semesters abroad and short term mission trips. I had been where few had been, and could talk about what most people knew nothing about. I was what I later laughingly called an "instant expert."

In 1976, I became pastor of The Church in the Gardens in Forest Hills, Queens, New York City. One day, while visiting an elderly parishioner in the hospital, I was asked if I knew Millard Fuller. Mr. Fuller, the parishioner told me, had just written a book about his missionary work in Zaire, the very country which I had just visited! Surely, we must have met!? Despite my ignorance and skepticism, the elderly gentleman gave me a copy of *Bokotola*, Millard's first book. In *Bokotola*, Millard told his life story: his business success, his conversion, his time with Koinonia Farm in Georgia and Clarence Jordan. Above all, he told the story of going to Zaire, taking a defunct brick making business and using that as the launching pad for what would become Habitat For Humanity.

Indeed, by the time I read *Bokotola* Millard had already returned, taken up residence at Koinonia Farm, and incorporated Habitat as a charity.

What did I think? Well, *Bokotola* was incredible. In other words, it was a great story and too good to be true. After all, I had just returned from Africa myself and I was already a leading expert on all things African! How could something so wonderful, so amazing, so miraculous, so spiritual, so brilliant, so clearly God-given be happening... and I not know about it?! Seriously, I actually thought that. And I pretty much wrote that to Millard.

Millard responded in his trademark way with a personal letter, and an open invitation, "y'all come down here, see for yourself."

God's Coincidences. I have no idea if Millard originated that phrase, but it certainly was central to his teaching. He didn't believe in blind luck, or happenstance, or coincidence. If something happened that brought things together in a way that helped, he called that "God's coincidence."

It was definitely a "God coincidence" that got me to meet Millard. Because of my mission trip to Zaire my denomination asked me to attend a meeting about Zaire in Atlanta, only three hours north of Americus, Georgia, the location of Millard's brand new Habitat for Humanity. I had never been to Atlanta, had no plan or desire ever to be there. Other than having seen "Gone with the Wind," I knew nothing of the city of Atlanta or the state of Georgia.

But I did know a "God's Coincidence" when I saw one.

So I went to Atlanta, attended my meeting on Zaire, rented a car, drove to Americus.

And fell in love. Head over heels in love. I loved Americus, I loved Koinonia Farm, I loved the Habitat idea, and I truly loved Millard. Even writing that sentence today reminds me of how true it was. I loved it all, and Millard at the center of it all. This was everything I was beginning to believe was *real* Christianity. By 1977 I was firmly convinced that mission, real mission, was the heart and soul of Christianity and of any healthy church. I absolutely, one hundred percent, believed the great quote from Emil Brunner, "the Church exists by mission as a fire does by burning."

My denomination at the time, The American Baptist Churches of the U.S.A. (ABC/USA), had done a superb job of teaching me what mission could be. Grassroots. Hands on. Personal. Humble. Partnership. In Zaire I had seen the American Baptist way of doing mission, and it was all of that. Suddenly, there I was in Georgia seeing the same spark, the same vision for mission – and Millard had a plan to take it across America and around the world, and into every church beginning with mine.

What did I see in Americus, and in Millard, that was so world-changing, earth-moving? Nothing fancy. Millard showed me eighty slides on an old slide projector. Even now I remember pictures of the brick-making machine on the banks of the Zaire River, and the first houses in Mbandaka. Then we went out to the first HFH house being built in Americus.

If I remember correctly, one house had already been built in San Antonio, Texas, so this would have been the second HFH house in all of the U.S.A.! – and I couldn't have been more impressed than if it was the millionth. It was the simplicity, the purity of it all. The house, just being framed, seemed to have a crew of two: a prisoner, just out of jail, and Millard. Building a simple, decent house, for a decent family in need. It just seemed so doable. And so right. So obvious. It was what Jesus would do.

I spent the night at Koinonia Farm, a few miles outside of Americus, where it all began for Millard. He often spoke with me about the rocky yet key role that Koinonia had played in his life. Some years before, Millard and his wife Linda, seeking a fresh path for their broken hearts and broken marriage and broken spirit, found their renewal at Koinonia. Koinonia was an interracial Christian farming community founded by the legendary Clarence Jordan. I had read Jordan's "Cottonpatch" version of the Bible in seminary, in which much of the New Testament was retold in the context and language of the Deep South. In Zaire I met missionaries who listened every Sunday night to old records of Clarence preaching and teaching the Gospel. Koinonia and Clarence were beacons of hope to Christians all over, and most especially to the Fullers at a very hurting time in their lives.

The Fullers stayed on, with Millard eventually leading Koinonia after Clarence's death. The seed of HFH first sprouted out at Koinonia when they built a community of houses for poor neighbors. That experiment hop-scotched to Zaire, and then back to Americus.

And there I was, with Millard, walking in the footsteps of Clarence Jordan, seeing the seed bed of Habitat, capturing the vision. I have often said that in 1975, before I stepped on the plane for Africa, I had never been farther away than New Jersey! By 1977 Millard and I were imagining changing the world with "a new frontier in Christian mission." One brick at a time, one house at a time, one family at a time, we were going to turn the world of Christian mission upside down by living the Gospel of Jesus Christ in such a practical, obvious way that folks could sleep at night at peace – in more ways than one.

In 1977 it all seemed so doable. For the next fourteen years we did it.

Part 2

My life with Habitat seemed God-ordained because I couldn't have planned it or plotted it. Even to this point in my story it was a dizzying string of God's serendipitous moments.

One morning, January 9, 1974, I read an Op-Ed piece in the New York Times in which the author said that millions were starving to death in Sub-Saharan Africa, and no one seemed to care. That horrified me and upset me, and led me to a conference at the United Nations Church Center on world hunger and apartheid...which led to my first mission trip to Zaire...which led a church member to give me Millard's first Zaire-based book...which led me to Atlanta, then on to Americus. Even I could feel that some hand was guiding events toward something beyond me.

The serendipity continued. Millard invited me to a HFH Board of Directors meeting in Dayton, Ohio, where I got to meet those early men and women who caught the HFH vision before there was anything to see. That was a key lesson. Lots of people are willing to jump on a bandwagon. Show people a success, folks will cheer! But for much of my Habitat career I was trying to convince folks that HFH could succeed long before there was anything concrete (no pun intended) to point to in their town or state or nation. In Dayton, I met folks excited about Habitat when it wasn't much more than an idea. I met one man who had two houses, and actually sold one to give the money to Habitat! Holy cow, I thought, people really do that? Really do that Jesus sort of thing, walk the extra mile, or if you have two coats and the other guy has none, you give up one for the other guy? I was meeting those kinds of people, people who were giving up their careers and money and retirement and security and comfort just to live the Gospel in a surprisingly practical way by building a house. So far all they had were a bunch of houses in a country most people had never heard of, one down in Texas, a half-built house in Americus, and Koinonia's initial experiment. But the excitement and commitment in Dayton were the spirit of victories already won, successes already assured, problems already solved. I saw confidence rooted in faith. That's a beautiful thing.

Millard once told an interviewer, "Our goal is to eliminate substandard housing from the face of the earth. Then we'll tackle something else." Early on, Habitat was built on people who believed that.

At the end of the Dayton meeting they needed a place for their next meeting. I offered my church, The Church in the Gardens. They also needed a Treasurer. God surely has a sense of humor to have let me be the treasurer of anything. Thus my journey began in earnest. Quickly, I was on the Board, serving as the Treasurer, and hosting it all.

In 1980 I was part of a team sent on a fact-finding trip to Uganda. On a layover in Nairobi, Kenya, my team members told me that I was to be the next President of HFH. Sam Emerick, Habitat's founding President, was retiring. I always assumed that I became President so soon because everyone realized how silly it was to have me as Treasurer, someone who knew nothing of finance. I felt like Pope John XXIII. It had been rumored that nobody much liked him or thought him competent enough, so they kept kicking him upstairs, and suddenly he was Pope.

Suddenly I was President of Habitat For Humanity. And in our minds, Millard's and mine and the Board's, that was a big deal. Because in our minds Habitat was a big deal. The world didn't know it yet. But we believed it. HFH has had a lot of slogans and catch phrases, but among my favorites was "a new frontier in Christian mission." We really believed that we were going to rock the world of mission. We believed that we were a refreshing wind to reinvigorate "The Great Commission," Jesus' call in Matthew 28 "to go ye into all the world, teaching all that I commanded." We were going to take that teaching to new heights, loving not in word only but in word and deed. We envisioned a world of Habitat houses, each house a little Kingdom of God, a little statement of faith, a little Word made Flesh, a little Gospel lived out in something we all need.

Another slogan I take some credit for is "building houses <u>with</u> people in need." I take credit for the "with." Whether intentional or not, early Habitat had often talked of building <u>for</u>. The preposition matters.

So I kept insisting that the word <u>with</u> be prominent in all we said, wrote, promised and did.

The decade of the eighties, my years as president, was my Habitat legacy. I can only compare it to my high school experience. I was a thirteen-year-old kid from New York City who found himself at The Mount Hermon School for Boys in very rural western Massachusetts. As part of its character-building education, Mount Hermon still had a working farm. With farm animals. One night it seemed like a good idea to go down to the pasture, climb the fence, hop on a cow. It wasn't a good idea, and it wasn't a cow. But it was a heck of a ride.

Presiding over Habitat was a heck of a ride. In that decade we went from being nobody to somebody, from something no one heard about to something everyone wanted to be part of, from the back page of a small town newspaper to the front page of the New York Times.

Easily the most important dynamic was Jimmy Carter's decision to jump into Habitat with both feet. That began innocently enough. When President Carter was defeated for re-election he returned to Plains, Georgia, only a few miles from Americus. One autumn we had our big Board meeting in Americus, to celebrate our roots and honor our relationship with Koinonia. It was a way to let Americus and Sumter County and southwestern Georgia feel some pride and partnership in what we were doing.

Millard and I thought it would be a great idea to have President Carter come by. Let me be clear. My idea was really tiny. I just thought it would be a kick to have a former leader of the free world drop by, say 'Hi', and sign a few autographs. That was the depth of my thinking.

President Carter offered to do more. He came to our meeting at the Presbyterian Church and really made a major address. It fell to me to introduce him and it is no exaggeration to say that I made a fool of myself. Made nervous by my hero-worship, I quite literally babbled before I finally mumbled his name. As he strode to the pulpit I tried to hide under a pew.

By the time Carter finished speaking my stammering was graciously forgotten. He spoke to us personally, intimately, and confessionally. I remember him telling us, "I've watched you from too great a distance," referring both to our fledgling Habitat and also to his decades as a neighbor to Koinonia. He had watched the hopes, the struggles, the boycotts, the people, and the faith "from too great a distance."

He offered to rectify that.

Millard, thankfully always the one with bigger strides, grabbed that offer and within days sent Carter a long list of the ways in which he could get involved. The rest is history.

Jimmy Carter was already a master carpenter, so a work-camp based ministry like Habitat was tailor made for him. And he kept his word. Very quickly he organized the first of many "Jimmy Carter Workcamps," and lent his name to our fundraising efforts.

The first workcamp was the world changer for Habitat. We were in *Losaida,* as it was known. The Lower East Side ... of Manhattan. For an idea that was born among the pecan groves of rural Georgia, Manhattan was some kind of change.

On Labor Day weekend of 1984, a busload of the heaviest southern drawls you ever heard rolled into Times Square where they turned a church basement into their dormitory. Then they went to East 6th Street to renovate an old six story apartment house.

I had actually led the first workcamp to that building, bringing a couple dozen teenagers from Massachusetts to spend winter vacation rehabbing, gutting the place. No electricity, no heat, no stairs, no windows. We had to use a fire escape very loosely connected to the building to get from floor to floor. All day we sledgehammered and crowbarred and shoveled, a couple of pastors and a bunch of very young suburban teenagers. No joke: a police cruiser came by and the cop told me I should be arrested for child abuse. She was not smiling.

But our little gutting paved the way for Carter's team to come in and truly build. That meant People Magazine, The Wall Street Journal, and NBC Evening News. People took notice. One thing people noticed was that Carter was serious,

Fuller was serious, and Habitat volunteers were serious. They worked hard, they worked well, they could preach the Gospel at morning devotions and act out the Gospel with hammer and saw all day long, sleep in a church basement to save money and live simply, and get up to do it all over again.

Habitat was made.

The rest of the decade was spent figuring out how to harness all the energy and people and money and hope that came our way. On the Board level that meant figuring out how to spend money right, keep our staff sane, keep the vision clear, and grow without destroying the Spirit at the heart of it. Millard was always reminding us of other ideas and organizations that had lost touch with their original vision. They may well have gone on to do good things in a new way, but the original purpose fell by the wayside. We were constantly trying to hone our purpose, to keep it front and center. This was important because the more we grew, the more folks wanted in, and the more we were pressed to defend our core principles.

That meant asking ourselves over and over again: what *is* a "simple, decent house"? How much "sweat equity" is too little, or too much? How Christian should this Christian mission be? Should we ask anything of local, state or federal government? What is our relationship with the local church? What do we do with families who fall behind in their payments? Do we include other religious groups and non-religious groups in our work, and how? And as for fundraising, how much is too much, and how much dare we spend on overhead?

These weren't just philosophical debates. I remember the first time someone offered us five thousand dollars if we dropped the "Christian" rhetoric in our literature, and the time Playboy offered us a lot more than that. Millard often

13

laughed that "the only problem with tainted money is there 'taint enough." But humor aside, he and we took each core issue very seriously. We weren't toying with a concept; we were wanting to stay true to a God-given idea.

One of the more heart-wrenching conversations happened when a Rabbi from Atlanta came to personally appeal that we intentionally open wide the door of Habitat to allow full participation by non-Christians. He meant something more than just agreeing to take the money from everyone or build a house for anyone regardless of religion. During my years, and I believe in the years since, HFH has done a good job of keeping Christ at the heart of Habitat and of opening the ministry in respectful and meaningful ways. That particular Rabbi probably felt he was up against a brick wall, but he began a conversation that led to genuine interfaith partnerships that respected the Christlike motivation of HFH.

The truth is we had a lot to learn, and the '80s were our learning curve. We were a mission, a ministry, a charity, a business, a housing company, a construction business, a church family, a development agency, a fundraiser, a publishing house, a volunteer agency, a headquarters, a franchisor, a brand. And most of it we learned on the run, the only speed allowed at Habitat.

Fortunately, most of our errors were errors of exuberance. One afternoon we were all set to launch a brand new urban project. We left our Board meeting dressed like Board members, and traveled to an empty lot on a busy street corner, a large bunch of mostly white people dressed in suits. We started to pray and preach, and were about to grab shovels for the official groundbreaking when our well-meaning holy circle was interrupted by a bunch of neighbors wondering who the heck we were, what the heck we were doing?

We had overlooked the neighbors. Live and learn, and we did.

We learned to work with mayors and unions and schools, with denominations and foundations, with celebrities and community activists.

Indeed, we were wonderfully naïve. We did walk in where angels fear to tread. I used to say that I could open the newspaper any Monday morning, see where the latest hot spot was in the world, and know we would be thinking of starting a Habitat project there. After all, we started in Zaire, and that turned out to be one of the more stable places we worked. Civil war in Nicaragua? Okay, let's go. Idi Amin overthrown in Uganda, rebels everywhere? Let's send David and three friends – if they come back alive we'll do it. "Shining Path" terrorists blowing up trains and buildings in northern Peru? Perfect place for a Board Meeting and work camp. Haiti in chaos? Great spot to work. Death squads in Guatemala? We can work there. Eastern Europe, middle east, Mexico City. My father once preached a sermon on "Faith and Foolishness." I always felt HFH had the right combination of both. Or put it this way, our foolishness was always rooted in faith.

That meant saying "yes" to Millard for his thousand-mile walk from Portland, Maine to Atlanta, "yes" to Armenia, "yes" to having Bill Clinton and Newt Gingrich as workers, "yes" to taking cancer patients on overseas workcamps, "yes" to setting goals no reasonable consultant would recommend, "yes" to building a village for lepers and counting their prayers as sweat equity, "yes" when all available evidence shouted "no."

"No" was not a word we used much.

15

It is hard to do justice to all these years without turning this into a five hundred page book with a million names and just as many stories. Millard was a master at that; I won't even try. The brief truth is that thanks to Habitat I got to go here, there and everywhere; speak, preach, raise more money than I ever thought possible; see towns and cities transformed; see churches and volunteers renewed in faith while getting blisters and splinters; "walk high in the cotton" as Millard said when we were among the movers and shakers of wherever we happened to be.

To paraphrase Dr. Seuss, "Oh, the people I've met, the places I've been, the lessons I've learned all thanks to Habitat!"

All in all I had thirteen years on Habitat's Board of Directors, the last nine as President. I don't know the statistics, but I seem to remember that when I began we had a $100,000 budget, and a house in Texas under the Habitat banner. When I ended it seemed like Habitat was everywhere, and money was rolling in. So it was a good ride.

I certainly benefited, enjoying amazing experiences with outstanding people, and stories that I will get into in the next chapters.

Chapter Three
Millard Fuller and Me

I slept with Millard.

What a cheap way to overreach for an eye-catching opening sentence. Millard was certainly one of the real transformative figures in my life. Charismatic, visionary, inspiring, prophetic. Those are all big words in religious circles, and Millard was all of them, and more. Provocative, challenging.

And I did sleep with Millard. That says a lot about my years with Habitat. My good old days. Long before celebrity endorsements and handsome headquarters and worldwide recognition, Habitat was a no frills, small budget, little mission. We were nobody. Just a few people with big dreams led by a tall drink of water from Alabama.

In those days, the late '70s and early '80s, the HFH Board of Directors met twice a year, fall and spring, usually in some place where a HFH project was getting started, where there was at least some burst of interest. Between meetings the Executive Committee and staff would meet, usually in Americus. That's how my love for Americus grew.

But this particular meeting was at Murray Branch's home in Atlanta. Murray was a spiritual giant on many levels. A renowned seminary professor, a Civil Rights veteran, a distinguished preacher, and, at the time, also the pastor at the historic Dexter Avenue King Memorial Baptist Church in Montgomery, Alabama where Martin Luther King, Jr. had pastored. Being with Murray was like walking through history. I remember one afternoon the doorbell rang. In came the pastor of the 16th Street Baptist Church in Birmingham, the same church where racist terrorists had killed four little Sunday School girls not two decades earlier. Looking at him, remembering those days, imagining the horror and rage, I wondered what I would have done as pastor of that church. Being in Murray's library in his home gave me the same feeling, that sense of history at my fingertips. Whenever I had a spare moment I went into his library and began to read at random, always assured of being challenged, inspired, or both. The chance to be with Murray and his wife, soaking it all in, reading his books, listening to him, working with him, made it a great meeting.

But, as Millard loved to say, at night the human race is all alike: we all want to sleep, safe and secure and snug in our bed. So our hosts pulled out the old convertible couch sofa bed ... and I slept with Millard. I can tell you this: he took up a lot more space than I with those long arms and legs.

But those were "the good old days." Habitat wasn't famous, we didn't have money, and every penny saved was one penny closer to a house being built somewhere. At the Branchs' house they cooked for us. In Americus we went to pot-luck suppers in volunteer housing. And we doubled up in beds. Traveled simply, lived simply, ate simply, and loved every minute of it. The good old days.

The best thing was that we didn't even think it was special, or noteworthy. It was just who we were. Stateside or overseas, we kept it simple. Sometimes too simple. Our Chaplains used to lead regional retreats for our overseas volunteers (later called "International Partners"). Staying in a little retreat center in Guatemala City, Guatemala, I got up early to take a shower. The instructions read: turn on the water, and connect the two wires above the shower head. That afternoon I learned that the contraption is called – for good reason – "the widow maker."

I kept track of all my speaking engagements from the moment I first returned from Africa. Everything from HFH slideshows to sermons to guest speaking and fundraising and HFH meetings. On an overseas trip I could well speak fifty or sixty times. During a Habitat event in the United States, it could be six or eight talks, radio interviews, television, and a Sunday sermon.

Even though preaching and speaking were my stock in trade, I learned a lot from Millard. He was a master at connecting with an audience. From homespun stories to Clarence Jordan-type Biblical teachings, from staying focused to wandering all over the place only to come back to the main focus, from remembering everyone's name to good humor to biting commentary, the man could speak.

One time he came to speak at my church in New York City. It was a Friday night, and we held the meeting in a small fellowship hall. I brought in an outstanding and large choir from a drug rehab ministry. They took up half the room. My church members filled the other half, with many standing. It wasn't long before Millard and I were bragging to the world about his "standing room only" event in New York City.

"David," he told me, "it's always important to pick the size of the room carefully."

Sometimes size doesn't help. A great friend, Rob DeRocker, was trying tirelessly to start a HFH project in the Lower East Side of Manhattan, in what is known as "Alphabet City," down near the Bowery, Avenue C and East 6th Street. Our plan was to blanket New York City with news about Habitat for a week. Every night, at some major church, we would present Habitat to a breathlessly waiting world! And I was the keynote speaker each night.

Twice, my mother and father were the only ones there. Once, even they skipped my speech. But Millard did not lose hope easily. He believed strongly that Habitat needed an urban presence, and New York was the media and financial capital of the world. He wanted that project, and by force of will it happened.

Millard liked to present himself as an old country boy. But he was quite at home among the sky-scrapers and power brokers, the politicians and bankers. And for the poor, the disenfranchised, the overlooked, he was in their corner whether it was the corner of East 6th and Avenue C, or the corner of some rural hamlet in Mississippi.

Another point we agreed on was to never turn down a speaking opportunity. Those good old days were packed with a lot of Rotary Club meetings, Sunday School classes, and shock-jock radio interviews called in from phone booths. Millard told me, "wherever two or three are gathered together, tell 'em about Habitat," paraphrasing scripture. My total ran to two thousand presentations before I quit counting. I can't imagine Millard's total. Millard would remind me that God puts in front of us the folks that need to be there. Though sometimes frustrating to hear, those words were usually right on.

Where I ended up always depended on Millard's availability, or Jimmy Carter's, or Andy Young's. Twice in my career we all spoke at the same event. Since I often put together the service, the first time I scheduled myself as the first speaker. Big mistake. Whatever I said was long forgotten by the time Young/Carter/Fuller had finished with them. The next time I batted fourth. Clean-up, they call it. Right.

I also had to get used to the way I was introduced. In Philadelphia, it went something like this: "We invited Millard but he couldn't make it. President Carter is in the

Middle East. Andrew Young is in Africa on business. Paul Newman is making a movie. And Tony Campolo was here last year, and he raised the most money ever! But we were able to secure this guy, David something-or-other. He's a pastor somewhere and does a little Habitat stuff. So let's give him a nice warm welcome." But I topped Tony Campolo in fundraising, for one night at least.

Two lessons I'll never forget. Once, preaching outside Baltimore at an historic church, I climbed a long, winding staircase up to a very high pulpit. As I reached one of the final stairs my eyes came directly, eye level, to a little sign beneath the pulpit. It read, "We would see Jesus." Yes, that's why folks were in church that morning. Not for a Habitat infomercial. Not for David's greatest stories. St. Paul said, "woe to me if I preach not the Gospel." That's why I was there, and that's why folks had come to the church.

Millard and I were lucky. We believed the Good News, the Gospel of Jesus Christ. And we believed that what we were doing was faithful to the Gospel, was "Good News," was obeying Christ's teachings. So, yes, we threw in good Habitat stories for illustrations, but we were always trying to illustrate the Gospel, to help people see Jesus.

That is why I never tired of having Millard preach in my church. Over the years I've had many guest preachers. Most all of them failed to preach. Instead, they would give a twenty minute advertisement for whatever project they represented. Millard never did that. He always came to preach the Gospel. He chose his scripture carefully. He respected the privilege of the pulpit, and he respected the audience. I heard him at Harvard and Yale, on city streets and rural farmland, in corporate headquarters and storefront churches. The setting didn't matter, the size of the audience didn't matter. The Good News mattered. The people mattered.

That was a tough lesson for me to learn. I had always been the kind of preacher to work tirelessly to develop a great sermon. But if it started snowing Saturday night, I put that perfect sermon aside; I wasn't going to waste the good stuff on a small audience.

Until one week I was back at my old seminary, Andover-Newton in Massachusetts, for a conference. The keynote speaker was Dr. Gardner Taylor, one of the greatest African-American preachers of the twentieth century. By mid-afternoon it began to snow, hard. At worship time, 7 p.m., next to nobody was there; there were just a handful of us. Yet Dr. Taylor proceeded to preach his heart out like there was no tomorrow. That night I asked Dr. Taylor why he did it, how did he stay so motivated and determined to give us few souls his best? "Because I never know if it might be your last day...or mine," he explained. If so, he was going to go out doing his best, I was going to go out having had one last best opportunity to accept the Gospel of Jesus Christ. Blizzard or no blizzard, if God put you up in front to preach you gave it your all. Gardner Taylor and Millard made sure I understood that.

Even when only five people were in attendance.

During a New York City HFH Board meeting, I drew the 8 a.m. service at a major Episcopal church in Manhattan. Now I'm sure there were multitudes at the 11 a.m. service. But at 8 a.m. there were five of us. Including me, the priest and the musician. But I had learned to preach my heart out. Millard and others before him taught me that. There are no insignificant worshippers. There can be insignificant preachers.

So I gave it my all. Not long after, one woman in the audience quit her high paying job, gave away a zillion dollars, took over the Habitat project, and later ran a homeless shelter for women.

What made Habitat so easy to be speaking about is that we really did believe we were changing the world; we really did believe that we were the new frontier in Christian mission. I will never forget one meeting in Americus. As I recall, it was a meeting of the Executive Committee so there were just a few of us. Millard had just returned from a trip out west and told us about an interview he had done. I've forgotten the question but I will never forget the answer. Millard told the interviewer – and he was telling us in Americus – that the goal of Habitat For Humanity was to "eliminate substandard housing from the face of the earth." And when we finished that, he said, we would tackle something else. I remember as clearly as I'm sitting here writing this that at that moment I understood that we were going to the next level, we were going into a gear with no limits, we were trusting God to work a huge miracle through us. There was no "maybe" in it.

This was not one of those, "Oh that Millard, there he goes again" moments. This wasn't Millard bragging or exaggerating. This was Millard stating fact, and we believed it. No hesitation.

It is often said, and I have studied it, that organizations in the first generation, led by the founder, are entrepreneurial in style. And that the Board is mostly made up of friends of the founder who really buy into the whole thing. That was true of these golden years, for good or ill. We may well have been sowing the seeds of our own destruction, but at the time we were all full speed ahead. We didn't let facts get in the way, or bruised egos, or hurt feelings.

The simple fact of the matter is that we were on a mission from God, to steal an old "Blues Brothers" line.

Seriously. Even in my very darkest hours with Habitat, even post-Habitat, I could still say with 100% conviction that Habitat was a God-given vision given to Millard. It wasn't just a good idea, or a cute idea, or necessary or urgent or helpful. It was God-ordained, and we jumped on to serve God in this unique way.

Now, we did try to rein Millard in from time to time. I pride myself on the fact that in my nine years as president we never tried to decide by majority rule. And we didn't rubber stamp for Millard. Whatever issue came before us we tackled with earnest debate and earnest prayer before reaching consensus. More often than not Millard won the consensus. We all looked forward to that one moment, like clockwork, after anything that could possibly be said had been said, Millard would suddenly stand up, take his southern drawl up another notch, and tell us how he saw it. I might have to spend a few hours later that night smoothing some ruffled feathers but most of the time he won us over.

The two constant difficulties with Millard were numbers and personnel. As a pastor and preacher I come from a profession notorious for exaggerating numbers, so it is hard for me to be too tough on Millard for exaggerating. I worked for a great pastor once who watched church attendance like a hawk. The ushers said if a dog walked by the church on Sunday morning and the door was open, the dog got counted.

Millard had a flexible relationship with numbers. We were always setting goals, especially on anniversary years (7th, 10th etc.), and it was uncanny how we always exceeded our goals. Even if some of the numbers for the houses built or dollars raised were backed up more by wishing and hoping than by concrete. At one of our big anniversary celebrations Millard's keynote address was focused on the difference between truth and fact. He never wanted facts to get in the way of the truth of what we were doing, which was modeled after the Olympic motto of faster, further, greater, more!

For the most part this type of preacherly exaggeration was innocuous enough that we could all wink, and head on to the next target.

The downside is that we were not much given to reflection; we did not often question publicly what worked and what did not. So we tried to learn from our mistakes without making it official or putting it in the minutes. For example, Habitat's marathon anniversary walks of seven hundred or more miles begged for reflection and serious analysis. Logistics, health and injury concerns, danger, recruitment, these were monumental tasks, and the folks who led these tasks wanted us to listen to them, learn from them. Millard was more inclined to be already thinking ahead to the next grand plan and not inclined to hear a discouraging word about something that was over and already a great success. Yet, without actually saying so we would do that reflection and analysis, and improve the next grand plan.

Personnel, sadly, was a sore spot. Especially during the first fifteen years or so, the HFH work was done by very underpaid staff, and by large numbers of volunteers who worked for a small stipend and lived in volunteer housing. Yet our expectations and demands on one another were extremely high. By its nature, then, HFH had huge and constant turnover as volunteers came and went. It was the pattern of life in Americus.

But the pattern was just as clear with staff. Good people, full of enthusiasm and faith and commitment, got hired by Millard, or Millard and a search committee. Soon enough I would hear grumblings from Millard about someone's work ethic, personal life, weaknesses, moral failures. It wouldn't be long until when that person suddenly "resigned."

When Millard fired me, he steadfastly ordered me to resign. "I have never fired anyone," he often boasted. I knew the game so I refused to resign, thereby breaking his streak of never firing anyone. It was my last chance to be first.

But up until that moment too much of my Habitat life was spent dealing with the broken hearts, the lost faith, the turmoil of good people beaten down by their HFH work experience. The problem in a nutshell was that Millard expected others to work at his pace with his single-minded dedication. I actually appreciated that. What Millard often would not see is just how hard and dedicated his people were. In my years with HFH, on staff and as president, I was never the first person to arrive at work, never the last to leave – and I'm an early riser and late worker. On Saturdays and Sundays, there were always people at work. Folks with responsibility for overseas HFH would come in the middle of the night to be in touch with overseas partners, and still be back to work that next morning, early.

Millard was hard on himself, pushed himself, and expected the most from himself. So he was hard on everyone else, pushed everyone else, expected the most from everyone else. The truth is, more often than not, that is what he got.

If you want proof that I'm an old fogey stuck back in the good old days, this story will do it. My favorite image of Millard was taking a walk with him in the neighborhood around the original headquarters. Trying to keep up with Millard was challenge enough, and I was a runner in those days. Trying to keep the conversation going was also tough because he bent over and reached down to pick up any piece of litter he ever saw. But even with the fast pace and the constant pick-ups, we kept a stream of consciousness conversation going. It was never nit-picking or complaining or gossip. It was never about sports.

It was always about the task at hand and the work ahead. By task at hand I mean that literally. As we walked down each street, a mile a minute, picking up litter, he would tell me about every household we passed, their hardships, their hopes, their faith. For Millard it was never about the house, it was about the family.

Early on in HFH history we knew it was time to have a "P.R. piece," a nice audio-visual to take on the road. Millard's old Zaire slide show was too dated. One year, with great excitement, we unveiled our official, new Habitat For Humanity media presentation.

To loud snores. We bored ourselves to sleep. Back to the drawing board. A few months later Millard sent us a new product. It was the story of one family in one shack on a street in Americus, and took us from them and their old front porch all the way to the dedication of their new HFH house in Americus. For my money that was pure Habitat and pure Millard in the good old days.

Millard didn't allow for setbacks. He didn't admit them, recognize them, or accept them. For him, any crisis was an opportunity. He even stated as policy, "create a crisis, find a solution." That was part of the fun, I think, finding a way beyond or above or through to whatever other side we were headed.

I hope the following is a true story. I heard it from Millard on one of our Americus walks and accepted it as Gospel. He showed me a house we were building to replace an abysmal shack. But whatever town regulatory board governed such things had determined that zoning wouldn't allow a new house on such a tiny plot. It was okay for the family to live in a tiny unhealthy shack, but not in a tiny brand new house. *Renovation*, however, was fine. So we renovated. We kept the old shack intact, built a new house around the outside, and as part of the renovation, of course, we needed to gut what was now the inside. I really hope that story is true because I've told it a thousand times. It sounds like Millard, and the Cheshire cat grin when he told it makes it true for me.

So, when all is said and done, who was Millard Fuller?

I'll keep it personal and not try for a universal answer. He was a great man who strode across this earth with big steps. Like a lot of things and people larger than life he was not always aware of the wake he left behind as he moved straight forwardly ahead. Maybe "wake" is a Freudian slip.

He was a visionary. I have never doubted that God gave him a specific calling to help the poor in a very tangible, basic, compassionate way.

And he was a good friend. As determined, as driven, as possessed as he was, when he was with me he was fully there. He could listen, reflect, wrestle, and not just on his turf, or on the things central to him. He was keenly interested in me, our family, my church, my kids' athletic careers, my writing.

Whatever his warts or weaknesses were, I always told him and anyone else that mine were worse. It so happened that it was my responsibility to look into his. He took it as his responsibility to squash me. He did his work more effectively.

But in the end I think Millard sold himself short in not believing that he could look at himself long and hard, and make some changes. He didn't need to deny and attack. He was a great and called man, with a genuine love for the poor. A little humility, a little self-deprecation, a little repentance and the ordeal that stalked him the last twenty years of his life could have been avoided.

I also think that his followers did him a disservice. When people told me they worshipped the ground he walked on, the Millard of my good old days would have cringed. When people tried to put him on a pedestal, the Millard of my good old days would have refused.

A last scene. We went to Jackson, Mississippi for a Board meeting. The last day we were taken away to some very rural hamlets, the epicenter of rural southern neglect. A local reporter told me that the United States congressman from the area took pride in how many unpaved roads he kept unpaved. Undevelopment was a policy there.

I remember Millard looking out across the field, looking at the shacks, almost feeling the barrenness and touching the despair.

"This can't be," he said to me. "This can't be."

My last good conversation with Millard, unburdened by all that was soon to turn us into Paul and Barnabas rent asunder, was in his office. He had been approached about getting HFH started in Selma, Alabama, being part of something big to honor and remember the pain and the triumph of that place. Should we do it, he wanted to know? Could we do it? It wasn't really a question. He knew we should and could. The author of *Bokotola*, a title about brokenness, the builder of Losanganya, a place about reconciliation, knew that Habitat belonged in Selma.

That was a lot easier than getting Paul and Barnabas back together.

Chapter Four

The Elephant in the Room

This is a touchy chapter. Because I'm not interested in settling scores or digging dirt. But it is disingenuous, and unfair to the reader, to ignore the obvious – a key part of the Habitat story for which I had a front row seat.

So let me make it short, and sweet. Around April 1 of 1991, I was fired by Millard Fuller. Thus ended my "good old days"! My unwillingness to actually dig through mountains of documents to pinpoint the exact date of this most traumatic event of my life is hopefully some proof that that event and all of its surroundings are not the heart of this story.

Frankly, I don't have the heart for that. Over the years I was offered money and opportunity to tell the inside story of Millard Fuller and Habitat and Jimmy Carter and all the sexual harassment charges and other failures of that era. At one point I had over two hundred pages written, good stuff, full of righteous indignation and the fervor of injustice, loaded with scriptures, and names, and a whole pile of revenge served fresh.

Eventually I had neither the heart nor the stomach for that.

I have rewritten this chapter a million times, imagined it a lot more than that. The last rewrite was at a coffee house in Williamstown, Massachusetts, a short step from Williams College. I knew the chapter stank at that point, and no amount of caffeine improved the chapter or my mood.

So I took a walk. All the way back to 1806. On the Williams College campus is a lovely sculpture nestled among trees, on obelisk topped by an orb. It commemorates a stormy day when five Williams College men took shelter by a hay mound, and committed themselves for foreign missionary service. That was the beginning of the modern missionary movement in America.

I sat there at the sculpture for a while, remembering the journey that took me to Habitat and, thankfully, beyond. I remembered what Habitat stood for and why I got involved. I remembered that Habitat really was a new frontier in Christian mission, and that this chapter should not undo that.

Then I remembered what it was like in the days after I was fired, and so many good folks along with me. Almost immediately we were encouraged to start our own ministry, just down the road, something Millard would actually do a decade later when he was fired after being caught up again in another investigation of sexual misconduct. We were even promised funding.

Not for one single moment did we consider it. We hadn't gotten into this mess to hurt Millard in the first place, and we were not going to end this by hurting Habitat. Our prayer, and it was prayed many times, was that Habitat would actually thrive, grow bigger and better than ever before, even without us. Each one of us remembered that we came to Habitat to serve, in answer to God's call. That was the hardest part.

Indeed, I went to Habitat, like so many others, in answer to a surely felt call, a calling to serve God, to engage in mission, and to help Millard.

Millard and I had a wonderful relationship. For several years we had talked about having me join the Americus staff. Encouraged by Millard and Linda, HFH directors, and by other staff, we would imagine a specific job, or creating a job.

Millard's extensive travel and speeches were overwhelming. I might help with that. Everyone knew of my devotion to the overseas work, so that would be part of my portfolio.

By the time I actually moved to Americus in January, 1990, Millard and I had been dreaming about that day for a long time. In many ways, moving to Americus was the culmination of my pastoral career. I never felt more ready, more called, more excited in my life.

The situation was this. I had been hired to be Director of Operations, an all-encompassing title that put me at Millard's side. In one form or another, I was responsible for our overseas work, our U.S. work, and another department or two to oversee in my spare time. It was heaven. Almost.

Just three months earlier, quite literally in my last hours as President of the Board, I had been informed of several allegations against Millard about his sexual misbehavior, advances, and touches toward HFH employees. These had first surfaced in some exit interviews with our Habitat chaplains. They brought these concerns to me as the outgoing President, and to the incoming President. Immediately, we formed a committee, along with the chaplains, to pursue this heartache wherever it took us. As a committee we found the women convincing and credible, and we had real fear for the wellbeing of Millard, for his marriage with Linda, for our integrity as a mission, and for each young woman who dared to speak with us.

Nevertheless, we were certain it would all go well. With that confidence I began the long drive, leaving behind the snow of Massachusetts for the warmth of Georgia. Storm clouds may have been on the horizon, but nothing could dampen my enthusiasm.

My mother is buried in a quiet cemetery in West Bridgewater, Massachusetts, her home town. As I began the drive to Georgia, my first stop was at her graveside. I talked with her, told her what I was doing and why, said a prayer and headed off to Americus. I don't know if it would be possible for anyone to be happier than I was. I was moving to a town I had grown very fond of through the years, to be with people I truly loved, to do work that I felt was life changing, world changing, peacemaking, vital, urgent, and God-given.

Again, I'm purposefully using words that might sound over the top. But that was the spirit of the day.

Later on, when all heck broke loose at Habitat, Millard's adherents would suggest that I came to Habitat at that precise moment in history for the sole purpose of getting rid of Millard, and taking over Habitat for myself. Such people clearly did not know me, did not know the feelings that Millard and I had for each other, did not know all the years of hopes and dreams we nurtured together about the future.

Naïveté is a wonderful thing. As are rose-colored glasses. And blind faith. I drove to Americus knowing that I had to sit down with Millard and confront him with some important issues concerning his personal behavior. To be blunt, I knew I had to get his attention, to help him to see that his sexual behavior toward many women over many years had crossed the line, that it was hurtful to the women, that it could be dangerous for him, and devastating for Habitat. I was not the first to say this to him. I would not be the last.

Sounds like a potentially explosive conversation, doesn't it! That's why naiveté, rose-colored glasses and blind faith are so wonderful, they make even the most odious task seem doable and likely successful. I wasn't worried.

Furthermore, I wasn't in this alone. We had an excellent sub-committee of the Habitat Board work on this crisis, the Habitat Chaplains were on top of it, we talked with several women, we thought through everything from legal ramifications to Millard's own feelings.

And we had a good plan. A loving plan, a kind and generous plan. We asked to meet with Millard privately, shared what we had learned, asked him to take a leave of absence, to enter into counseling, and to be guided by a team of spiritual elders of his own choosing.

Sounds reasonable. It seemed that way then, in 1990. Still sounds good today. From my perspective, I had a dear friend doing a lot of risky behavior that was hurtful to others, threatening for the ministry, and dangerous to himself and his own family. The plan was private, and even kept fall-out to a minimum. The women weren't asking for anything. We invited Millard to take the leave of absence in conjunction with a book tour to promote his new book. The "spiritual elder" idea was very popular in evangelical Christian circles. The idea was that if a Christian leader got into some sort of a problem (moral, financial, personal, sexual, addiction, etc.), rather than just condemning them, firing them, "tossing them under the bus," the real goal should always be healing, redemption, reconciliation, restoration.

For us that meant that the real goal was to have Millard back in Americus, leading Habitat as soon as possible, with a renewed focus, a stronger marriage, and a clearer awareness of his own weak spots. All to the good.

Or not. Rose-colored glasses are quite fragile. Millard denied everything, refused every offer of help, disparaged the women, and even added additional names. One by one he tore apart the character of each woman: "this one is crazy" ...

"that one came after me" ... "she is unstable" ... "it was only a kiss." One by one he added to our list.

By the time the next year was over, and I was freshly fired, I had the names and stories of a lot of women, way more than we began with, going back to his Koinonia days.

But we didn't bring all those names and stories to Millard, or to the public. Our goal was not to humiliate Millard, or even to build a case. Our goal was to help him, and in helping him to also help his marriage and his Habitat For Humanity. In football they talk about "piling on." You have the opponent's ball carrier on the ground, but more and more players keep jumping on him, "piling on." Or people use the phrase "push their face in it," as a way to make somebody squirm, or feel humiliated, or defeated.

That wasn't us. We did not pile on or push his face in it. We were just a few long-time friends of Millard hoping to save Millard from himself. What's more, we thought it would go smoothly! Three Christian men, sitting down with a dear Christian leader, offering to help him with a problem that was dangerously out of control, and to do it all with no publicity, completely confidential, with a process run by friends of his own choosing.

Stupid us.

In short order Millard denied everything and demanded the names of the women, made it all public, brought the whole Habitat Board into it, and got the press involved. The full Board ordered Millard out of the headquarters for a year, and into counseling, and then developed a reconciliation plan. The one hundred and fifty or so people staffing the Americus headquarters were soon choosing sides; people began betting their careers on which side would win, loyalty reports were made, and everything was set in motion for the day of Millard's return.

In the meantime, the reconciliation plan was full speed ahead. Covenants were made promising no firings, no recrimination, and no purge of those who believed the women.

Stupid us.

If this was a book about the 1990-91 sexual misconduct crisis at Habitat For Humanity, I could go on and on ad infinitum, or rather, *ad nauseam*. But this is only a chapter within the larger and much better story of one of the world's most innovative and caring charities. In fact, the images and stories that come to mind are more about human nature than about scandal.

I remember, early on, hearing that Millard had written a letter of apology to the first group of women. When I saw the apology I knew immediately he hadn't written it – it was too short! I said to him, "Millard, this letter isn't *you*. You write long letters even to small donors; you even preach long. You've never done anything in your life in a few sentences!" We were still capable of laughter at that point, and he smiled and admitted that President Carter had written it. Carter confirmed that to me later.

The months ahead would be haunted by rumors: Millard apologized, Millard recanted, Millard admitted to some but not all his misdeeds. People tried to discern what an 'apology' would mean, and even wrote more for him. Nothing got settled.

The sorry truth is that we were all trying to come to grips with something most of us could never imagine happening, or that some us had hoped would never reach such proportions. Some tried a reasoned approach, using this crisis as an opportunity to reach out to Millard and beg him to face a whole range of management style issues – issues of leadership and decision-making, of prejudices and quirks – that had been swept under the carpet for too long. Millard was reminded that respected senior staffers had tried for years to get his attention about his treatment of women in particular and of his co-workers in general.

Meanwhile, backlash was virulent, nasty, and aggressive, against me, the women, the chaplains, or any who hoped for the women to be respected and treated fairly. I was told that I was demonic, Satanic, and in league with the devil. As a group we were all lumped together as "northern liberals and feminists" staging a coup to get rid of fundamentalists. It seems silly to write these things today, but at the time lives, careers, families, and ministries hung on whether such silliness was believed.

For those of us who were certain that such silliness *could* never be believed – well, stupid us.

Of course, what most everyone wanted was for things and life and HFH and work and friendships to be back to normal. So people tried everything, good, bad and ugly. One of Millard's best buddies, caught in a complete lie, told me, "I couldn't help it. I just love Millard so much."

Soon enough, Millard's supporters organized a boycott of HFH. People stopped sending funds. Local U.S.-based Habitat affiliates withheld their tithes, their ten percent of funds raised that not only supported the headquarters but all of our overseas projects. One by one, I called these boycotting affiliates. Those were heartbreaking conversations. I knew some of these folks. They loved Habitat, they loved Millard, and they loved the overseas work. Some even liked me. Some even shared our concern about Millard's treatment of women. But as one long-time Millard friend said, "I worship the ground he walks on." They refused to end the boycott and send the designated funds until Millard was fully restored to leadership, with a guarantee of no more investigations.

The efforts within HFH headquarters were more formal, probably well-intentioned, but completely worthless. Countless "reconciliation" meetings were held, with or without mediators present, at which I was the official spokesperson for ... for what? Over months of meetings I was requested to represent the women, or the committee that had investigated, or the HFH staff, or the community within the headquarters that wanted justice, a fair hearing, and no recrimination. The meetings were formal or informal, with the HFH Board or Board representatives, at Millard's house or at the Carters' home in Plains. I flew to Washington, D.C., and Harrisonburg, Virginia. I drove to Florida and South Carolina and Atlanta. There was even a mandatory, all-day sexual harassment seminar for all HFH employees. People tried.

With 20/20 hindsight I can see clearly, and state un-equivocally: not one good thing came out of any of it. I have referred to my stupidity repeatedly, and that is not an attempt at self-deprecation or false humility. It's simply that as I write all this, so many years later, I am genuinely amazed at how stupid I was. Call it naïveté, or innocence, or faith, it still smells like stupidity.

It was just after Easter, 1991, when finally I was called into Millard's restored office and fired. Soon, a lot of people, some of Habitat's most treasured workers, were also fired.

Needless to say, all heck broke loose. In the twinkling of an eye all that we had imagined Habitat to be was gone. Community. Friendships. The Kingdom of God in action. Gone. Instead, we were just another corporation going through downsizing. Without a heart. Like the Tin Man we were in our own world of Oz, and as in Alice's Wonderland everything got "curiouser and curiouser."

Someday someone should do a case study of how HFH handled its first real crisis – or even the later one when Millard finally fell from power in 2005. In my days we tried the best we knew how. We consulted experts on sexual harassment, P.R. people taught us about damage control, and we hired the Mennonite Conciliation Service. We even prayed. But vengeance won out.

Naturally, those who were not fired were happy, or relieved. Many of their heads would roll later on once they had outlived their usefulness. Each side had its symbols. All over town there was a sudden appearance of black flamingoes in honor of those fired. In response, the non-fired folks papered the headquarters with little drawings of a house with the words, "the only thing that matters." No people in the drawing. That wasn't the Habitat I recognized.

The death of all this wasn't as quick as anticipated. It dragged on. Habitat's Board was shocked and angry, the press was on it, and the nationwide and worldwide HFH network was as upset by this latest turmoil as they had been by the original mess.

To my amazement and relief I was officially told not to worry. The Board's chair and committee chairs assured me that the Board would overturn the firings at the upcoming Board meeting. I reassured everyone. I was told not to appeal, not to seek counsel, not to go public or protest, not even to attend the Board meeting at which our fates would be determined. No need to even defend myself. Not to worry.

I obeyed.

Stupid us.

Late one afternoon the Board president called from their meeting, informed me that I could not be reinstated. They had just fired Millard, and they didn't want one side to look like winners. So all the firing stayed, plus Millard joined our happy unemployment line.

For about a day. The next day Jimmy Carter went public, threatened to withdraw from Habitat if Millard wasn't restored. Everybody agreed that was a lovely idea, and Millard was back on top.

Me? And the others? We were still fired. Habitat didn't want it to look like a deal was cut, so they stood firm – against those they had promised to protect. Covenants be damned.

The next few months were a textbook case of something, but I don't know what. People who were happy with the firings said that it was about time that HFH got more corporate. Forgiveness, reconciliation, turn the other cheek were passé. Time to get tough. I learned that there is nothing uglier than a Christian mission deciding to get corporate, and end up being neither Christian nor corporate. One Board member with a successful career in finance reminded Habitat that in her corporate world, when there were a lot of layoffs, the corporation turned most of a floor over to the people, and provided phones and career advisors and support staff.

We were just shown the door. Literally.

Crises teach a lot about human nature, and humans, some of it disturbing, some inspiring. It struck me, for example, that HFH was the perfect storm for a sort of theological conundrum. Evangelicals, too many at least, have a weakness for worshipping individuals. Liberals tend to worship a cause. Habitat had both, a big individual in Millard and a big cause in housing. The end result was that the evangelicals did not want to see Millard hurt, and liberals did not want the cause of low-income housing hurt. The rest of us were expendable.

Nevertheless, the Habitat headquarters was a mess, with people laying low hoping not to be fired, or lining up to prove their loyalty, or just going about the work they loved hoping not to get caught in anyone's drama. For a few months, while the fired people remained in town, it could get messy. Unfriendly encounters. Awkward silences. Outright hostility. Gossip.

One of my keenest disappointments was how quickly the local paper became the head cheerleader for Millard. They never grasped that the people he fired, abused, and harassed were Americus residents, taxpaying neighbors, with kids in the local schools, who shopped in the local stores, played for the high school teams and band. We were them. Instead, the paper seemed to buy into Millard's propaganda that we were all "northern liberals." Northern Sumter County, maybe.

The hardest part was the goodbyes. The fired Habitat people, including volunteers making $25 a week in food money, were all people devoted to HFH's goals. People had sacrificed careers, high paying jobs, and security in order to work in the shelter of a Christian ministry in order to shelter the world's poor. Many literally felt called by God to take the path to Americus. Now they were told to move on, get over it.

In the weeks before the massive firings, a "house church" sprang up as a faith home for many Habitat workers. We kept the house church going throughout the worst of the turmoil, as a place of healing and faith and encouragement. The toughest spiritual question was this: what do you do when God calls you to do a work, but others prevent you from doing it? How do you just move on when you know full well that God intended you to be at Habitat? It wasn't just another job. It was ministry and calling and faith in action and answered prayer and mission all rolled into a job.

But, all good things come to an end. Right? Sometimes with a little push. Day by day, people moved on and away, most thriving in new adventures. And all wondering, what if?

As for me, I was lucky. I got a good lawyer. I knew where the bodies were buried, so to speak. So in short order I had a two-year severance package, allowing me the chance to rebuild my life while my son finished Americus High School.

Meanwhile, I needed a life. I immersed myself in my son's athletic career at Americus High, something he handled with good humor. In the fall, Aaron was the only member of the Cross Country team, so we drove every Saturday to road races all over kingdom come. My real salvation was his high school baseball career. From spring training in January to summer ball through August, I could structure my life around his life, which I did to excess. The miracle is less that I survived HFH, and more that my family survived me.

A family joke, not entirely untrue, was my threatened hunger strike. As my unemployment wore on and the rejections piled up with the black balling more obvious, and with my severance running out, I announced to the family that if I did not find a job in time I would begin a hunger strike to the death on the sidewalk outside Millard's office. No one tried to talk me out of it. That may say more about how pleasant I was to be around than about their faith that I would find a job.

All kidding aside, it took the two full years of severance to regain my career as a pastor. At one confrontation with Millard out at Koinonia, he accused me of "being on Habitat welfare, stealing money from the poor, depriving the needy of decent housing." He may have believed that. The day he fired me he promised me "two or three months' severance" since he was so sure I was marketable after my outstanding Habitat career! Instead, I was damaged goods with a suspicious firing from a major charity whose reference was a terse "we can only confirm that Mr. Rowe was employed here from January 1990 until April 1991." Behind the scenes, off the record, much worse was said. Whether from an active smear campaign or a Nexus search of newspaper articles, I was suspect.

I knew my goose was cooked when I interviewed for an excellent, thriving Baptist church. After they narrowed down their final choices to me and one other candidate, they said to me, "We have no problem with your Habitat firing. We all work in New York City, we know all about power plays. Some win, some lose, no problem." No surprise, I came in second. "Power play" was one of Millard's favorite explanations for what we northern liberals were really up to.

I felt like Bill Murray in the film, "Groundhog Day." Every day I got up, and my new job was to find a job. I applied for over one hundred jobs, mostly churches, and quickly discovered that my name was mud. The Habitat world I had helped to build turned out to be pretty big, and I kept bumping into it.

There were a couple of attempts at reconciliation. On one occasion I was offered a senior position back at Habitat if I would denounce certain other Habitat workers, and blame the whole Millard/sexual harassment fiasco on them. Millard, himself, wanted no part of reconciliation. Not until I moved out of town, he told me. Later on there was a rather humorous attempt at reconciliation, arranged by a mutual friend. The humorous part is that it ended when Millard sent me a letter by mistake, meant for someone else, making clear that he had no desire to be reconciled, that he was just playing along.

Forced unemployment also forced me into a lot of self-reflection, analysis, questioning. Some things became clear right away, some took time, and forgiveness took almost forever.

I did know that I wanted to return to being a pastor. For months I was haunted by the verse from the Book of Revelation in which Jesus faults some followers for forsaking their first love. Being a church pastor was my first love. After a reckless and somewhat sin-packed youth, my conversion was rather dramatic, and my journey to pastoral ministry was quite intentional. I love it. Despite noble motives for joining Habitat it was still true that I had forsaken that first love.

My severance also granted me travel money, so every few months I hit the road looking for a job, desperate. I wasn't desperate to get out of Americus, we really liked it there. But I was desperate to know that I could work again, that I still had it. Each rejection convinced me that I had lost it. After a while you wonder if you ever had it.

Desperate, I sent out résumés unsolicited, I knocked on church doors uninvited. I called in favors and leaned on friends, I grabbed guest preaching spots anywhere, anytime. God's timing was not anything I understood. Patience was never one of my virtues.

Work: that I understood. What the heck, I decided to write a book about work. Being an early riser I had a lot of hours to fill. While finding work was Job One, I also started writing.

My first book was more of a booklet, *Something Small For God*. It was a first attempt to tell the story of the little mission I had started in India, Friends of Christ in India (FOCI) in 1983. When I moved to Habitat I essentially suspended FOCI, and this booklet had a two-fold purpose. One was to revive FOCI, to get it up and going again. The other was made clear in the title: *Something Small for God*. Believe me, those of us who were fired and many still within HFH spent hours, days, weeks trying to understand what went wrong. Clearly, the problems were deeper than Millard's misbehavior, or the Board caving in to Carter's threats, or organizational sycophancy winning out over principle.

My title hinted at one theory, that perhaps it is possible to get too big, that maybe there are problems which become inevitable when institutions, even good institutions, get too big. We didn't know this to be so, we were guessing. Certainly our HFH experience pushed us toward that theory.

From our earliest days, Habitat was very aware of all the classic pitfalls that can trip up new, growing organizations. On the Board and staff levels, we discussed this all the time. Habitat was a first-generation entrepreneurial style organization. That meant that we had a visionary, charismatic founder who was still in charge, surrounded by a hand-picked Board who loved him and bought into his vision. Such groups and such leaders are high gain/high risk, and we rode the gain to great success, and we weighed the risks. We studied the literature, we planned for the future, we imagined a second and third generation of leadership, and we initiated term limits on the Board and Board recruitment. Even the worst of what we faced, this crisis with Millard, was not a surprise. Aside from the actual names and details, nothing in this episode was unexpected. His personal behavior, interpersonal behavior, tenacity, revenge, foibles, preferences and prejudices were well observed, often discussed, and feared.

Yet we were not prepared. We failed. We failed institutionally, organizationally, spiritually, pastorally, personally. We failed. I failed.

My little booklet was a very humble attempt to learn something. Printed cheaply in India, perhaps two thousand copies, it ostensibly told the FOCI story as a way to reintroduce that mission and start raising funds. But it also was an appeal to smallness, to not lose focus or purpose in a grab for growth. As our dwindling group of fired friends continued to meet, we found ourselves returning to that theme. We were committed, as we went forward with our lives, to working in ways that would not ask us to sacrifice principle or faith or integrity for gain or popularity or success.

My next book was an even more direct result of the HFH fiasco. Being *out* of work helped me to focus on what I loved about working! *Faith At Work* was not a book about Habitat; it was meant to be a theology of work, even an ode to work. The original title was *Theology of the Hammer*, and it was accepted and contracted with that title.

Millard wasn't done with me, yet. A year later Millard decided to write a book with the same title and using the same little Macon, Georgia, publisher! What a coincidence. The publisher determined that the phrase "theology of the hammer" belonged to Millard and in short order his book came out first – with my title.

Still, I had fun with the book, doing mailings and workshops and retreats, and celebrating the gift of work. Best of all, the process of writing a book kept me sane while I pondered the irony of writing a book about work when actually out of work. I do believe that unemployment focused my attention on the joy of employment.

I am sure that the life of a writer added to Millard's anger toward me. Each day found me on my front porch with a cigar in my mouth, or at the bar of the Windsor Hotel with a tequila at my side, writing. Eventually, I gave up both.

What I never gave up was thinking. A lot of my self-reflection focused on my Habitat life. What had gotten me to this point? Fired. Smeared. Desperate. Where had it all gone wrong? What could I have done different? What could Habitat have done different?

The truth is that I blame myself for much of what went wrong in those "good old days." I was on Habitat's Board of Directors for thirteen years, President for nine. No one was in a better position to know Millard's weaknesses and Habitat's. We had a great and open relationship. We were in constant communication, even about difficult and unpleasant matters. Yet I could not prevent a looming disaster.

Millard, by his own admission, had a long history of broken relationships with colleagues, staff, and Habitat workers. When he fired me he reminded me that he left a long string of broken bodies behind, but the work goes on. Back in the '80s, after another crisis caused by another firing of another Chaplain, in exasperation I said: "You keep firing good people, and you say it's always their fault. One of these days, we'll have to look at you."

We never did. Not really. The truth is that we loved him too much, and we loved Habitat too much. That love would come back to haunt us when the whole mess erupted in 1990/91. No matter how much evidence we had, no matter how many women, no matter how many Habitat covenants were signed and promises made, people loved Millard too much, and Habitat too much, to stand up.

In contemporary counseling language, I was the chief "enabler," and I set myself up for the fall. And I never learned.

What often happened is that internal crises and employee complaints, even from senior and long-term staff, would reach a crescendo. This was before emailing, so I would receive urgent phone calls. Or on my many visits to Americus I would be called into offices, taken out to lunch, invited over after work to hear another litany of problems with Millard. And always sworn to secrecy: "Don't tell Millard." "You can't use my name." "It can't leave this office." "But I know you can help." A fool's errand on my part, to take in everyone's grief and complaint, to promise confidentiality, and to expect to effect change without using any information that could be traced back. Everyone feared retribution, or joining the ranks of broken bodies. They were smarter than me, obviously. I just went on, thinking that a little nudge, a little hint, or a little heart-to-heart between two good friends would return Habitat life to the little corner of The Kingdom of God that we believed it to be.

Sure, we tried some things. One year we gathered the entire Board of Directors and all senior staff for a long, intensive retreat in the woods of Comer, Georgia, at Don Mosley's Jubilee Partners. Jimmy Carter recommended and paid for some high-powered and talented management consultants to guide us through to the Promised Land.

My job (I keep telling you I was stupid) was to take that ongoing cycle of Millard-complaints, all the dis-ease, discomfort, disillusionment, disagreement and lay it all out in my opening devotions. In effect, I was to speak for everybody without anybody owning up to it.

That stupidity prepared me for greater stupidity during the sexual harassment crisis of 1990/91. At that time the Americus Headquarters was so divided, after Millard went public and began to counterpunch, that Habitat brought in a Mennonite Conciliation team. False advertising. The only real thing about them is that they were Mennonite. They did nothing to accomplish conciliation. And their idea of teamwork was to hang me out to dry.

At least four times I was ordered into hostile meetings with Millard and Linda Fuller. Let me repeat: I was ordered. It was like the moment in *Mission: Impossible* in which a tape recorded voice always warns, "Your assignment, Mr. Phelps, should you choose to accept it ..." and then always concluded, ominously, "should you get caught we will deny any knowledge of your activities." That was me: *Mission: Impossible.* I was ordered to represent the interests of those concerned about Millard's mistreatment of women, and to do it alone. In some of the meetings we at least had the presence of the Mennonite Conciliation team, providing some pretense of objectivity.

The final meeting, however, was a doozy, and it once and for all sealed my reputation for stupidity. I was to go to Jimmy Carter's house in Plains, Georgia, to meet with the Fullers and Carters. The Fullers and Carters were dear friends, fellow church members, joined at the hip as future events would show. I was to go alone. No colleague, no advocate, no friend, not even the Mennonite Conciliation team. Just me. If I refused to go it would be held against me, officially. If I did go, I was way out on a limb by myself. "You're being set up for the fall," the Mennonite leader warned me, "and we can't help you. You have to go, but you have no recourse if it doesn't work." I lived the old proverb, "damned if you don't, damned if you do."

I preferred to be damned for doing, so I went for a fascinating afternoon. The Carters were gracious hosts, the meeting somewhat whimsical and nostalgic, the result deadly.

Mr. Carter offered a hopeful suggestion, based on his historic Camp David Agreement between Sadat and Begin, Egypt and Israel. He talked about the need to be generous in confession, and generous in forgiveness. Specifically, for reconciliation to be achieved, one party must confess to even more than they truly think they're guilty of, and the other party must forgive even more than has been confessed. The key is that each side is generous, in confession and in forgiveness. I would confess to even more than I thought I was guilty of. And I would forgive even more than I thought Millard was genuinely confessing.

I loved it. It was inspiring, the light at the end of the tunnel. It was humane, it was Christlike, and it was generous. Let's do it! Shake hands, get back to the work we love. Man, that was easy! Why didn't I think of that? I loved it.

Millard refused. Period. End of story.

My biggest disappointment was the failure to create real forgiveness and reconciliation institutionally, within the whole ministry. That is what was really needed, not just something between Millard and me.

After I was fired, before all the other fired folks moved away, while there was still time, I said to anyone who would listen that Habitat had the chance to write a new chapter in Christian history. Christianity is full of breakups and divisions and hostilities and back-stabbing. There's no news in that.

Millard, in defending his firing of me and a lot of other colleagues through the years, loved to talk about the split between Paul and Barnabas in the Bible. Of course, he got to play the part of Paul!

But I challenged HFH to rise above two thousand years of Paul and Barnabas breakups, and write a story of healing, forgiveness. True reconciliation. Everyone unfired, back to work, together.

That would be news.

Oh, well.

That really was the end of my relationship with Millard. A couple of nasty phone calls or chance encounters that ended badly. A few faux reconciliation attempts when his career hung in the balance. I even introduced him at an event for our local HFH in Bridgeport, Connecticut. We said pleasant things about each other, proof that he was right: sooner or later everyone comes back to Habitat because it is good.

Chapter Five
Americus, Georgia

Amerigo Vespucci is mostly forgotten. A long-ago explorer, his name lingers on thanks to a map seller who attached Amerigo's name to the continent. It then became part of these United States, and lent itself to the town of Americus, Georgia. That's what I heard. Truth is, it was what was going on in Americus that got me to see more of America.

Americus became one of my favorite parts of the good old days, an unlikely favorite part. I can say both that I am New England born and bred, and that I grew up in New York City. Both are true, and both are a long way from rural, southwestern Georgia. But I liked it from day one.

In my mind's eye Americus is much more than a small town in southwestern Georgia. It gave birth to my whole experience in rural Georgia. Brilliant yellow fields of mustard, pecan groves, Kudzu sculptures enveloping miles of trees, endless fields of bright white cotton, deep fried anything, peach everything, boiled peanuts, heat, red clay. And picturesque shacks. And people.

From 1977 to 1993 Americus was very much the center of my universe. Habitat board and committee meetings, crises that arose from time to time, interviews, they all provided a good excuse to go south. I liked it so much I always tried to come early and leave late.

What was the attraction? The fact is it grew on me, it expanded like the circles after you throw a pebble into a pond. My first association in Americus was Millard Fuller and his law office in a small, pleasant, quaint house on

Church Street. It seemed like Mayberry. By the time I loaded up my rented Ryder Truck to move away sixteen years later I was leaving home, and the only house I ever owned, and friends, neighbors, bartenders, librarians, church members, a school system I really admired, a way of life I liked, colleagues, warmth, gnats, and memories.

In between, Habitat expanded just as my Americus circles expanded. Year by year HFH bought up houses all around Millard's law office, transforming that neighborhood into a HFH community. The houses became home for long and short term volunteers, guest quarters for work camps and visitors, office space for the growing staff. A stone's throw away in every direction were Habitat houses replacing shacks, or shacks soon to be replaced. The end result is that whenever I was in Americus I was in a growing neighborhood of friends, people whose lives were touching mine and whose lives I was touching. And since I really did assume that Habitat was forever, Americus felt like my true home. Most of my life had been lived in transit, moving from school to school, church to church, and state to state. Wherever I was I never expected to be permanent. In my mind Americus was my permanence. For my first ten years with Habitat I expected to keep visiting forever. When I finally joined the staff, I expected to live and work there forever.

Again, what's so special about Americus? At the risk of sounding sappy, Americus/Sumter County/Koinonia, this was the earth that gave life to everything I really believed in. Christianity as it should be. Mission as it should be. Volunteerism as it should be. Community as it should be. Even Bible Study and worship as it should be.

What made all that "as it should be"? A lack of conceit, of arrogance. We thought what we were doing was important, but not at someone else's expense. Our "theology of the hammer" could be summarized by one doctrine: let's get to it. Someone is in a shack, someone is in a mud hut, someone is sleeping under a bridge, someone wants to break out of their cycle of poverty, someone wants to hold the nail while I hammer, someone else is ready to saw if I'll hold the board, someone will lay the brick if I'll mix the mortar. We all had just about enough energy for doing that all over the world. We didn't have extra energy for all the other stuff that people get into that divides folks, drains enthusiasm, causes fights, saps energy, and gets nowhere. We stayed focused.

In my thirteen years on the international HFH Board I don't remember any fights. People had opinions, even strong opinions, on everything. Homosexuality, Biblical inerrancy, Just War vs. Pacifism, capital punishment, politics. But nothing took our eye off the ball; nothing took priority over our humble effort to do our little part in building the Kingdom of God.

Here's the real scoop on Americus. May I make a bold and outrageous statement? We really, really believed that we were building the Kingdom of God. Yes, I have capitalized that and I mean it. I also learned the hard way what a bold and outrageous statement it is. Just for the record, outrageous does not mean it is wrong.

Years earlier, fresh out of seminary, I joined the staff of a great Baptist Church in Haverhill, Massachusetts. Their interim Senior Pastor was a legendary retired seminary professor who allowed me to get my feet wet by preaching occasionally. One Sunday I preached on our role in building The Kingdom of God. The next morning he called me into his office to correct my heresy. He told me that human beings had nothing to contribute to The Kingdom of God, that this was entirely God's domain and God's doing, and that God needed no help from us. He had taught my father in seminary twenty five years earlier, which led him to conclude the conversation (and his call for my resignation) by offering to "call (my) Daddy, and we'll settle this out nicely."

I stood my ground professionally, theologically and Biblically. God wants our participation in the Kingdom of God, and the Kingdom of God is not just "pie in the sky, by and by," it is for the here and now. Didn't Jesus tell us to pray, "thy Kingdom come, thy will be done on earth as it is in heaven"? God expects some "sweat equity" from us on his Kingdom building as surely as HFH expects sweat equity from Habitat homeowners. The price of admission is our participation.

In fact, aside from Millard's book, the first published Habitat resource was a book I co-edited, *Kingdom Building,* a collection of essays on the work of HFH written by many of that first generation of Habitat enthusiasts.

Yes, walking the streets of Americus, living and working in Americus, immersing ourselves in Americus, being in Americus seriously, intentionally, literally seemed like we were significant builders of the Kingdom of God. There was an evangelical spirit combined with social action, a combination much under attack nowadays. But it was a breath of fresh air when we were at it.

At the risk of oversimplification, for much of Christianity's history people and churches had been divided into two camps with different priorities: evangelism or social action. Evangelism was telling people about Jesus. Social action was doing what Jesus said to do. One or the other. We wanted to do both. We were comfortable talking about Jesus, and we were determined to take his dare seriously to make a difference in the daily lives of "the least of these." That is what made it feel like Habitat was Christianity as it should be. I could feel that at morning devotions, at a worksite, at a board meeting, or at public events. And in Americus I felt immersed in it. Clearly I had some hero worship going on, plus idealism and the rose-colored glasses.

The rose-colored glasses worked. I liked the people, the weather, and the scenery. I liked shopping at the Piggly Wiggly, the best named supermarket in the world. I shouldn't admit it, but I liked that anything could be deep fried. Pickles, okra, ice cream. I liked that the whole town slowed down for Sunday mornings and Wednesday evenings, when church took priority. I liked that, despite whatever the local history was with race and class, we were all among each other all the time and things were changing. I liked the idea that anything you tried to do really could make a difference.

Above all, I liked the feeling that Americus was the centerpiece of Habitat as clearly as Habitat was increasingly the centerpiece of my life. My ministry, my career, my family life were immersed in HFH. Throughout my children's high school and junior high years summers often meant a Habitat work camp trip to Peru or India. Winter break and lots of Saturdays were given to work camp experiences in the northeast. Camaron accompanied me on lots of speaking engagements. Key figures in Habitat history stayed in our house, spoke at my kids' schools, preached in our church. We were a Habitat family, through and through. Moving to Americus just made it more obvious.

In Americus it felt like everybody was living my Habitat life. I am sure it wasn't so, and time would prove that rather convincingly. But it sure felt like it when I visited there and when I lived there.

Whenever I visited Americus I spent the daylight hours going from office to office, visiting people who had hitched their wagons to the Habitat star. There was no difference between the $25 per week volunteer and the senior staff;

both worked hard and gave it their all. Often they had left lucrative jobs or secure career paths in order to make sure that some family somewhere had a chance at a decent house. Everybody I dealt with minute by minute had a stake in making that happen. At lunchtime Millard and I would head up to the center of town to a local restaurant, greeted always by townspeople proud of what we were up to. The churches of Americus got more and more involved with us, hosting all sorts of Habitat-based events. The Methodist and Presbyterian churches were early encouragers and public partners. As our presence grew in Americus, we were more deeply engaged in everything from local schools to local theater to local softball leagues to local churches. It felt like Habitat was at home in Americus.

Nowadays, some of HFH has moved to Atlanta, a move mocked by the Fullers at the time that it happened. For the record, it was Linda Fuller who first spoke to me about moving the headquarters, back in the mid-'80s. Rightly concerned about Millard's exhausting travel, and a six hour round trip commute to the Atlanta airport, she asked me to quietly consider moving closer to Atlanta. I did, we did, comparing labor costs and housing, weighing pros and cons. Our heart wasn't in it. We liked Americus. So we stayed. It was home.

Increasingly I thought maybe it should be my home. Millard and I had talked about my joining the staff for several years. A rising tide of need and urgency and opportunity and several of God's coincidences made it happen. It may have had something to do with turning forty. In 1987, as I headed toward my fortieth birthday, I prayed to God that God would let me use my life in changing the world. Turning forty impressed upon me that life is finite and time is fleeting and people were hurting and I did not want to waste a single moment. As president of Habitat I was on the cutting edge of world mission, the cutting edge of development, the cutting edge of church work. We can argue about whether that is true, but I absolutely believed it. And Americus was the heartbeat of it; it was where everything emanated from. Again, that may or may not be true, but I believed it to be so. That was the theological reason behind accepting Millard's urgent request that I move there. It seemed like a good idea. It seemed like God's idea.

Jumping into Americus with both feet only confirmed my feelings. By 1990 Habitat for Humanity was a large, thriving, growing, popular, nationwide and worldwide ministry, and Americus was the physical and spiritual and programmatic center of it all. I knew everybody, had a hand in hiring most if not all of the senior staff, and many people were longtime personal friends. I don't think there is anything in my life that I approached with such confidence and joy.

That first year of living in Americus was as close to heaven as I could imagine. It wasn't easy. The whole Millard drama was alive and kicking but somehow it did not consume our days or warp our work. The very nature of Habitat's work kept us on our toes. Building houses in countries all over the world, and in towns all across America, assured us of excitement, challenge and opportunity every day. We lived for that.

My job was Director of Operations. In effect, I was number two to Millard. Specifically, I was in charge of our overseas work, our U.S. work, and a couple other departments. It was never boring. With the break-up of the Soviet Union there were chances to work in Hungary and Armenia. The garbage workers in Cairo wanted a HFH project. Despite coups and famines and death squads and civil war, we still had building blitzes in Nicaragua, workcamps in Peru, college spring break teams in Haiti, new opportunities on the Mexican border, we approved a thousand-house project, Asia was beckoning.

Meanwhile, all of our various kinds of Habitat workers scattered across the world were facing every imaginable crisis, opportunity, joy and sorrow. Late night phone calls and early morning faxes revealed the depth and breadth of their lives. Our Chaplains, Paul Davis and Julie Peeples, made sure that those workers felt as close to us as if they lived next door.

At the same time, it felt like we were as American as apple pie and baseball, sprouting up everywhere. College kids and senior citizens, RV caravans and motorcycle clubs, unions and pro sports teams, Miss America and aspiring politicians, TV anchors and Hollywood stars all joined the legion of good-willed American citizens willing to turn a free Saturday or a vacation week into "the American dream" for some hardworking family.

This was my daily life. And every moment of it was lived with people I loved, admired, respected. Even the folks who ended up stabbing me in the back were folks I had enjoyed, hired, promoted, and protected.

One guy was so awful that when we had to make some cuts even his friends begged me to fire him. I kept him. Later, when I measured the knives in my back his was the biggest. Turns out he was, in truth, a paid informer, and Millard's top spy. This in itself led to some humor. I was a big coffee drinker, and kept a coffee warmer on my desk. As the day wore on I would turn it on or off many times. Later it was reported that the coffee warmer was really a secret tape-recording device that I used to gather evidence against Mil-

59

lard or incriminating conversations from suspected friends of Millard.

Despite the intrigue, and the silliness, the work stayed simple, focused, and vital. All over the world folks counted on us to stay at the top of our game. Somewhere, some family's hope and future well-being depended on us. That commitment never wavered.

I only lived in Americus for three years, and for two of them I was fired and unemployed. That means that the bulk of my experience there was as a plain old everyday citizen. This had its humorous side. Shortly after my son got his driver's license he was pulled over for a traffic violation. By then, all the uproar at Habitat and my firing had played out prominently in the Georgia newspapers. In fact, in one inadvertently honest moment, Millard had told an interviewer that I had been fired for being "a defender of women." (Now that <u>did</u> look good on my résumé, and I did use it!) On this particular day of my son's traffic mishap, Aaron and I appeared before an unusually friendly judge with a particularly low opinion of Millard. Once the judge confirmed that Aaron's father was *the* David Rowe, his court case was resolved.

Once I was fired, my Americus relationships fell into three types. There were the HFH people and Millard supporters who despised me. There were the Americus citizens who didn't like Millard and/or Habitat, who wanted to shake my hand. Both groups were rather small. Ninety-five percent of folks didn't know or care. This was incredibly liberating and led to one of the most interesting eras in my life. For two years I was mostly known as "Aaron's Dad."

This may have been one of the best lessons for me. Up until that point, I divided Americus into two worlds. There were the pro Habitat people and churches and pastors and streets and beneficiaries, the people who liked Jimmy Carter or Millard Fuller, the folks who worked at Habitat, local and otherwise. And then there was everybody else whom I assumed didn't like Habitat or the poor or New Yorkers or black people or mission. I was that dumb. I did learn better.

In my two post Habitat years as a simple citizen of Americus I had all my prejudices and assumptions and stereotypes challenged, thank God. Just as I was stripped of my veneer as Habitat big shot and turned into just another neighbor, my neighbors became real to me.

Americus High School became my window into the real world of small town America in the deep, rural south. All the issues we may pay attention to sociologically or politically were played out in real time in the hallways and on the playing fields of the high school. You name it—race, class, poverty, literacy, parenting, religion, even agriculture—I had the privilege of a front row seat to see it all played out. And I had the time to enter into it.

Aaron jumped into life at Americus High School even more thoroughly than I had jumped into Habitat. Despite the turmoil, drama and uncertainty that my choice created, he has always been grateful for those years, experiences and friendships.

I don't pretend to know or understand the racial history of the rural, deep South in a place like Americus. What was obvious is that most white kids did not go to Americus High, leaving the local public high school mostly black, seemingly neglected and viewed apathetically. Aaron loved it, and provided me with two fascinating windows into my new hometown.

First, he was a baseball player in a town where baseball was King. They played in a huge, all wood, historic stadium maintained by prison labor. Parents and friends gathered in the stands not just for spring and summer games but for every minute of every practice from February through August. That is a lot of hours immersed in local gossip, local culture, local religion, local economy, how the crops are doing, will the local shirt factory close, what church is splitting in two, who beat up who, what family is going broke, who needs help.

I had come to Americus to take part in a sort of intentional community. I found it in the stands of the Americus High baseball team. Together we solved the world's problems, helped each other over the humps of life, cheered on each other's kids, and confronted the insidious evil of racism in our own small ways. Sometimes humorously. Sometimes spiritually.

One day there was an altercation on school grounds, one student called our center fielder a "nigger," punches were thrown, the white student went to his car and got a knife, the fight was broken up, and the center fielder suspended. So one boy uses the "N-word," starts a fight, and has a weapon on school property. The other, our black centerfielder, is suspended.

The next day at practice, sitting in the stands next to some school official, I suggested that our player be reinstated immediately, or I would call my brother, the sports writer for *The New York Times*. He was reinstated. I don't have a brother.

More profound was the rivalry with another high school that surprisingly featured an all-white baseball team. Over the years and in several games against that team my son, a second baseman, would be called "a nigger lover." In the stands the parents of the other team would extend their sympathy to us for our kids having to play with "niggers."

This racism and hostility grew game by game, year by year, carrying over to chance encounters at the mall or Wal-Mart or McDonald's.

I was stunned and inspired by our players' resistance to such evil. This led me to break a lifelong rule. In all my life as an athlete, a coach, a parent I never once prayed for victory. I didn't believe that God was needed to take sides in a game. But in Aaron's senior year, before that last game against that bitter rival, I prayed privately and in church that God would bless Americus High with victory as a sign of God's approval for the way our players dealt with all this.

Yes, we won. Sometimes the good guys do win.

Aaron's high school life led directly to a request that I start a local chapter of the "Fellowship of Christian Athletes," FCA, a nationwide campus based ministry. The whole issue of religion in public schools is still muddled. But as I understood it, if students wanted an organization, and they could find a non-school adult to be the Advisor, and it was held before or after school, and there was no coercion by staff or coaches, then a religious club was acceptable. Coming from New England this was a shock to me.

Even more shocking was to have scores and scores of teenagers show up for Bible Study and breakfast at 6:30 a.m. in the school library, or at night after practice. Football players and cheerleaders, tennis players and Aaron's baseball teammates, marching band members and just plain friends showed up month after month to bring Christian faith face to face with all they faced each day. "The thrill of victory, the agony of defeat," injuries, sitting on the bench or being cut from the team, peer pressure, parental pressures, drugs, alcohol, sex, cheating, we looked at it all through the prism of Christ and scripture. It was amazing.

A radio station heard about our group and came by to interview me and a couple of participants. One of my athletes was a three sport star, and he was asked why this group, why his faith, meant so much to him.

"When I score a touchdown, people cheer. When I hit a winning basket, everybody loves me. But when I strike out, or miss a shot, or drop a ball, people can turn on me quick. With Jesus I always know that He loves me, no matter what I do, even when I mess up." That was his answer.

So, to my surprise my move to Americus ended up a brutal disaster, and yet I still ended up with a delightful community and a very special ministry far away from my ex-popularity at Habitat Headquarters! God, indeed, has a sense of humor, of timing, of purpose. Anything to keep me sane.

Of course, HFH was never far away. For almost two years we had a "House Church" in our living room every Sunday morning, one of the best worship experiences of my whole life. Free form, shared leadership, no budget or bylaws or structure, creative, open. And composed of all Habitat people, past and present. This, too, led to profound and humorous exchanges. After one "House Church" service, a young female Habitat volunteer complained of continuing sexual harassment, so I told her to speak up.

"And end up like you?" she said, with no touch of sarcasm or irony or insult intended.

Living there day after day put me and Habitat in each other's way more than either of us wanted. There were months of negotiations for my severance, fits and spurts about reconciliation. But far more likely were the chance, daily encounters, good and bad. As I walked down a street I saw a Habitat friend of many years heading toward me. When he saw me he crossed the street to avoid me. In the

Piggly Wiggly grocery store old Habitat friends walked out of the store rather than share the aisle. I continued to play in pickup basketball games at the Presbyterian Church playground. One afternoon the man I was guarding threw the ball right at my face from a distance of about two feet. "How could you do that to Millard," he screamed, "I just love him so much."

Truth is there were a hundred times more nice encounters than nasty, not only with Americus folks in general but with the ongoing Habitat work force. Many of Aaron's friends were children of HFH staff. Our House Church was made up entirely of Habitat people. Habitat people offered many kindnesses, from a simple friendly "hello" to tickets for the Atlanta Braves, from invitations to preach at their church to letters of introduction and recommendation, from prayer to a nice front porch visit.

Bottom line? I always loved Americus, still do. It was at the heart of some of the best times, and helped get me through the worst time. For a big city boy, small town America had a lot to teach me. It really was a microcosm of America, all of our hopes and ideals and virtues side by side with our hurts, failures and shame.

In 1977 I drove into Americus for the first time. In 1993 I drove out for the last time. My last day in town I took one of my favorite long runs. Hot heat, endless fields, wooden shacks, a million memories. It was shacks that got me there in the first place.

When I use the word "shack" I don't know what it conjures up in your mind. A poor person's house? Substandard housing? Depending on your standard, substandard isn't very descriptive. Like a mud hut with thatched roof in rural Africa or India, a shack can conjure up something quaint and picturesque, even traditional or historic. Unless you live in it.

When I first started visiting Americus I would see these shacks and say to myself, "why, that must be left over from..." and I would be about to say, "Civil War days." Then I would see movement in the shack, someone on the porch, smoke from the chimney. People lived there. Ate there. Made love there. Did homework there. Dreamt there. Died there. Not so quaint. Or picturesque.

You see, I thought they were treasured relics, preserved for tourism, like red barns and covered bridges and fieldstone fences in New England.

No. These were real houses for real people in real time.

A shack. Little wood structure. Some tar paper. Broken down, left over what-have-yous in each room. Precarious. Unhealthy. Sad.

Symbolically, emotionally, I let the shack serve as a stand in for the hovels of the world, all the places where some family was trying their best to live their lives with hope.

And it was the Habitat of southwestern Georgia, of Americus, of red clay and cotton and pecans, that helped move that hope along.

I saw that hope come alive in a Sumter County shack.

My starkest shack memory was in Plains, a few miles outside Americus. Millard and I went there one afternoon to tell a family that they had been selected to receive the first Habitat house in Plains. The family were tenant farmers; they got to live in the shack in exchange for working the farm for the landowner. The dad made $65 a week, plus the shack. The shack was full of rat holes and roof holes and floor holes. When we told the parents about the Habitat house, the Dad leaned up against the wall, a dangerous thing to do. He praised God, thanked us, and begged us not to tell anyone until the house was finished because he was sure the land-owner, a Deacon at a local church, would evict them right away. The Deacon did find out. He did evict them.

While talking with the parents, a young girl came out of the bedroom. She overheard our conversation. She asked me if I wanted to see the picture she had been drawing and coloring of her "next, next house?" Notice, it wasn't her next house, the Habitat house, it was the next, next house, the one she would live in after the Habitat House.

She showed me.

It was the White House.

That's why I was in Americus. That's what drew me to Millard and drew me to Georgia.

Chapter Six
Africa: Zaire-Congo and Uganda

(Note: In telling my story, I will generally refer to The Democratic Republic of the Congo as Zaire, the way it was known when I was there.)

Cursed.

Whether you call it the Congo, or Zaire, or the Belgian Congo, or Joseph Conrad's *Heart of Darkness*, the place still seems cursed. I don't believe that, but it can seem that way.

I haven't been to the Congo since 1981. You could not have convinced me then that that may have been the high point of Congo/Zaire's post-colonial, independent development. Even then it was chaotic, troubled, divided, and wracked by poverty and civil war, a pawn in Cold War Soviet vs. U.S.A. politics. Zaire was slowly being devastated by the as-yet-unnamed AIDS epidemic; it was the birthplace of "blood diamonds," and it was ruled by a ruthless tyrant who single-handedly spawned the idea of a "kleptocracy" – government by stealing.

Then things got worse. Zaire, even with the fall of Dictator Mobutu, became known for the Ebola virus, and a blood lust of such cruelty that newspapers failed to describe it.

Yet it is impossible for me to remember the Zaire of my days without joy. My first love affair was with Africa, and it began in Zaire. It was a miracle and a combination of "God's coincidences" that got me there for the first time in 1975. The year before I had read an article about famine in Africa, and it left me stunned, actually disbelieving. From my little rural church in upstate New York, I set out to understand a humanitarian crisis that was beyond understanding. That led to a conference on "Famine and Apartheid in Africa," which led to a mission trip that was to include Zaire, Kenya and South Africa.

At that time in my life I did not have a nickel to my name or any prospect of finding a nickel. But I signed up for the trip, seriously feeling an inexplicable call to go. One day a dear elderly shut-in from my little church died, with my name on her lips. Her family was so touched that they gave me a check for the exact amount necessary for the trip. Part of the miracle is that I had not told anyone of my plans. Yet, it seems, God was not only pulling me to Africa, but pushing me.

So off I went.

I was a fairly naïve, provincial person in 1975. Perhaps you have seen the famous New Yorker Magazine cover that shows a rather warped world map. There is a gigantic rendering of Manhattan that fills up most of the map, then there's New Jersey, and the rest of the world is faint at best. That was essentially my world view. I was a New Yorker first and foremost, with just enough New England in me to round off my accent. Everything else was more than foreign.

Three weeks in Africa changed all that. This was my introduction to the world of mission where faith and courage, love and sacrifice, vision and pragmatism all lived close by.

Barbara Kingsolver's novel, *The Poisonwood Bible,* is a provocative and sweeping novel of missionary life, brutal politics and international intrigue set in the Zaire of the 1960's. Though I found the book to be historically accurate on many levels, I still yearned for it to have included the kinds of people I met. The missionaries and Zairian church leaders I met were folks of enormous compassion and a generosity of spirit, and they forever changed my life and the shape of my pastoral ministry.

Zaire would also turn out to be my introduction to Habitat. Little did I know that Millard, fresh from missionary service in Zaire, was back in Georgia preparing to launch HFH, building on his Zaire experience. For me that was still two years away.

In the meantime, my Zaire experience was marinating me, changing and challenging my views on just about anything.

One story may summarize this whole seminal experience, and provide the link to HFH.

It was Thanksgiving Day, and we were way out in "the bush," not quite jungle but not Kansas, either. Our hosts did a lovely job of preparing a Thanksgiving dinner as near to the classic American feast as they could. At the end, an American Baptist missionary named Gene Gentry asked if I wanted to go for a ride. We hopped on his dirt bike, and thus began my Ph.D.-level course on what modern mission can be. As we rode deeper and deeper into the bush, on paths that weren't identifiable as paths, heading for a remote village, Gene told me a story. Gene was an agricultural missionary. His calling was to share the Good News of Jesus Christ within the context of helping subsistence farmers improve their farming. That could mean teaching the value of crop rotation, or planting on a hill in such a way that erosion won't kill your soil and stop your crop, or changing from the short-handled hoe to a long-handled hoe.

Or taking care of your chickens. Gene had grown weary of trying to tell subsistence farmers what to do. A subsistence farmer is exactly what it sounds like, a farmer who ekes out just enough from his little land to put enough calories into the family to last another day. Subsistence is a step below existence. It is the bare minimum. When you can't see past today, it is hard to change.

Gene stopped trying. He decided to concentrate on farming his own land, trying "best practices" with his own farm which included chickens. He took care of his chickens, built a coop, fed them, cleaned out the coop. As people walked by the mission compound's little working farm they could judge for themselves. Maybe Mr. Gentry was just another pushy American with no respect for traditional ways. Or maybe he knew something.

Mankwela was a subsistence farmer, lurching from crisis to crisis, trying to survive. He saw Gene Gentry's chickens, Rhode Island Reds, fat, healthy, meaty. He wanted to buy some. Gene's offer was too good to resist. Mankwela could buy a chicken for, say, $1. Or he could have them for 50 cents if he agreed to allow Gene to show him the proper care and feeding for plump, meaty Rhode Island Reds. He knew a good deal, and took it.

This is not as easy as it sounds. The "care and feeding of chickens" was not in the worldview of rural Zairian subsistence farmers. They assumed that chickens exist to serve man, not man to serve chickens! The idea of housing, feeding and cleaning up after – incomprehensible, not the natural order of things. Unless you want delicious and productive chickens.

That's why I was on the back of a dirt bike careening through centuries to visit Mankwela.

One of the paradoxes of mission work is the unsettling combination of beauty and poverty. Eden could not have been more beautiful than the trip to Mankwela's village. Par-

71

adise won't be more beautiful. A green canopy overhead, gentle hills, idyllic, quaint mud huts with a hint of smoky fires.

And hunger. Tattered clothes. Distended bellies. The almost red hair of malnutrition.

We rolled into the village, greeted immediately by Mankwela and his family. The village chief came to formally welcome us, sending a young boy to shimmy up a nearby palm tree to retrieve a gourd of palm wine, a ceremonial toast to thank God for what God was doing through Gene and Mankwela.

Before we drank our explosive palm wine, we poured an Old Testament-like "drink offering" onto the ground, thanking God for bounty and blessing.

When I recovered from the wallop of the palm wine, I was taken to the chicken coop as Mankwela told us his story. He had endured a lot of derisive abuse when he started doing things Gene's way. People mocked him when they saw him bending over to feed his chickens, or climbing into the coop like a chicken himself to clean it out.

Now there was no mocking. Mankwela was the pride of the village, the chief said, "bigger than me," he laughed, truthfully. The chicken farm was now feeding his family, and his kids sold eggs door to door. There was money for more chickens, extra money for school fees and medicines, and nutrition in the bellies. Other farmers took notice. Maybe planting in rows across the hill instead of up and down is not so silly. Maybe letting the land rest for a season, maybe trying new crops, maybe the longer hoe all make sense.

And maybe the other story the missionary farmer talks about, the story of God's love in Jesus, makes sense, too. Worth a listen.

What has this got to do with Habitat? This took place two full years before I was to even meet Millard, see him in action in Americus, and hear about this tiny new mission with the absurdly lofty goal of eliminating substandard housing from the face of the earth.

But Gene and Mankwela were already teaching me the essentials of HFH – partnership, sweat equity, pride of ownership, capital not charity, humility, the Gospel hand in hand with action, word and deed together.

That very morning, in deepest bush Zaire, I had also seen the polar opposite of Habitat. Another missionary asked if I wanted to see "the cemetery." Sure, another window into local culture, I thought. He took me to a huge warehouse, like a Quonset hut. Inside was a huge array of modern farming equipment, tractors, spreaders, and combines: everything a farmer in Kansas would want. But as I said, this wasn't Kansas. This was a place of no gas, no gas stations, no spare parts, no mechanics. This was a place that was thinking about trying a long-handled hoe, and being nice to chickens. But in one of the sillier examples of Cold War politics, China had flown in by helicopter a veritable John Deere Showroom. The cemetery.

Two examples in one day. The old way of mission, top down, paternalistic, inappropriate. Or the new way, Gene Gentry and Mankwela, "the new frontier in Christian mission," as Millard came to call it. Americans and Zairians, Americans and Nicaraguans, Americans and Indians, volunteers and homeowners, just plain folks working together, sharing wisdom, loving one another as they wished to be loved. No big deal, except it is.

Gene and Mankwela weren't the only ones understanding how to plant right. By the time I returned to

73

America, I was fertile ground, I was ready for the seed Millard was starting to plant.

That germination was and is ongoing. I am still learning how to do mission right, pastoral work right, ministry right. But Gene and Millard sped up my learning curve. That learning curve included further trips to Zaire and Uganda on behalf of HFH, the two countries I feel I got to know a bit. I touched down in other places, spent a few days here and there in Kenya, Tanzania, and Zambia. I never did get to South Africa; they banned me twice which enabled me to form my own opinion about apartheid. It is Uganda and Zaire that were my windows into Africa and world mission, and my first big steps with Habitat.

It is impossible for me to remember the Zaire or Uganda of my early days without joy. What is that, a paradox, an oxymoron? It is not nostalgia. I certainly saw the worst that they had to offer, but everything I saw was within the context of faith, of hope, of love, of the Gospel. It is second nature to live joyfully, hopefully, lovingly when Christ is at the heart of what you stand for. I am not trying to sound like a preacher. I am trying to explain the inexplicable.

You will have to take my word that I am not naïve or Pollyannaish. It is simply that I am constantly confronted by a Gospel far more powerful in its joy than evil is in its rottenness.

I well understand that people find that uncomfortable, even insulting. Throughout my ministry I have had to fight the urge to cringe whenever people like me experience grinding poverty and return to report how happy, cheerful and religious everybody was.

For years I took my youth groups to Habitat projects all over New England, plus New York City and Jersey City. They saw tough lives. They fed the homeless living in the bowels of Grand Central Station, and in drug-haven city parks. Across the street from HFH's first New York City project, on the Lower East Side, there was a most fascinating homeless village built on an empty lot. The "residents" were drug addicts well versed in the housing philosophy of Buckminster Fuller. They knew how to do a lot with not much. Their little village was a network of refrigerator cartons, laid on their sides, lying on top of scrap wood planks and purloined garbage bags. In other words, insulation. This was mid-winter. Our young people visited the residents, ate lunch in the cardboard village, listened to "scared-straight" harangues against drug abuse (and urban politics, gentrification and a few other issues).

Yet my youth groups returned home talking about the joy and faith and happiness of the people they met.

At Greenfield Hill Church we have sent youth and adults to Appalachia every year for over thirty years, where they work with the Appalachia Service Project, another housing ministry. They get to know the families they help, they play with the kids, and they learn about black lung disease, they see rural poverty face to face. Yet they can't help but report about all the joy, the smiles, the faith they see every day.

When I think back on my experiences in Africa, I do feel uneasy remembering the good, the positive, and the joyful. Logic says it shouldn't be. Yet faith makes it so, I don't know how else to explain it. Despite famine, tyrants, and genocide, faith still wins.

I got my comeuppance on this subject during a stay in Uganda. My denomination got me into Zaire, and Habitat got me deeper into Zaire, deeper into Africa, especially Uganda.

By the early '80s I was writing my doctoral thesis on *African Traditional Religion and Christianity* under the legendary and beloved Orlando Costas. Costas kept me humble and focused, reminding me kindly that I really knew nothing. Africa is too big, too complex, too removed for me to read a few books, drop in a few times and think that I understood. My "instant expert" days were long gone.

But HFH gave me experiences of Zaire and Uganda, and with that a glimpse of Africa. Those experiences and glimpses were immersed in faith, suffused with faith, impossible without faith.

Don't worry, I'm getting to my comeuppance.

When Habitat was invited to start in Uganda, that in itself was a miracle. Uganda's notorious dictator, Idi Amin, had tortured the nation for a decade before being overthrown. When we arrived in Kampala, the capital, Uganda was in the chaos of euphoria and revenge. Teenage soldiers were everywhere, roadblocks and check points appeared out of nowhere, roving militias made each day feel like Russian roulette.

Our little team of four Habitat people served either as advance scouts – or bait. At the HFH Board meeting where we were asked to start HFH Uganda somebody actually said, "send David, if he comes back alive we can start." It is true that we were there to see if it was safe. It wasn't.

Our host was a dynamic Ugandan pastor, Kefa Sempangi. He had escaped Amin just ahead of the executioners, but returned to help rebuild, and was the Minister for Housing. Widows from Amin's rampages convinced Kefa to bring HFH to northern Uganda. That was our destination. But first we settled into our high-rise, once-upon-a-time five star hotel. No water, no elevator, no food, no toilets. Just us.

One night, sitting on a balcony outside our room, we heard gun fire all around us. When it occurred to us that our room light was the only visible light around, we dove for cover and prayed for morning.

We made it to Gulu in northern Uganda, near the border with Sudan, defying fate and death more than we dared to admit at the time. Over the course of several days we faced crocodiles, malaria, rebels, snakes and horror stories way up close and way personal. One morning I attended worship at a Catholic church, a thousand widows and me, a thousand women whose husbands had been murdered, and me.

Later we went to a remote village and met the woman whose story led to the following poem: *"The Wonder Widows of Uganda."*

I once met a woman
who had to eat her husband.
She was from the wrong tribe
the wrong tint
 the wrong land
the wrong language group
the wrong something or other
driving sanity undercover
making madness O.K.
while wives wiped the tears and taste away.

Some ancient hate, Godless fate,
Devilish ruse,
forced her to choose between her children's lives
 and her husband's corpse.
To stay in power, of course,
rulers must rule
with ruthless abandon
driving a stake through hearts of hope

> *making evil seem invincible*
> *and life a cruel joke.*
>
> *But that motherwifewoman pulled through,*
> *a miracle of ancient faith grew*
> *a testimony of Greater Power*
> *spoken of by the wonderwidows of Uganda*
> *in epic, Biblical terms,*
> *like Daniel in the Lion's Den*
> *and the furnace that could not consume his friends.*
> *With courage greater than sorrow*
> *They lived to build tomorrow.*

The poem is all true, the beginning and the end. The heartache and the faith. My meetings with Ugandan widows were the most embarrassing and inspiring meetings of my life, and gave me my comeuppance. My miniscule faith in the midst of their gigantic and truly-tested faith, my being overwhelmed by what could not overwhelm them, my Bible as a pulpit prop compared to their Bible as a foundation stone ... all this took my breath away, shook me, and turned me around. Listening to the widows school me about Daniel and the Lion's Den, and Daniel's friends in the fiery furnace, was my comeuppance. How could I question their joy, their survivorhood, their hopefulness, their almost giddy optimism, if I really knew my Bible?! They really asked me that, with humor and exasperation. Okay, I got it.

If Gene Gentry and Mankwela were my mentors in Zaire, a little girl was my mentor in Uganda. Those days in Uganda were awfully hard. I hate to admit it, I'm not proud of this, but I began to feel sorry for myself. I know, that makes no sense, but it is true. Uganda was so hard, so close to the evil that had run amuck, that all my sympathy and empathy got used up.

I had met too many widows, too many orphans; heard too many stories of bodies floating down the river, clogging the dam; seen too many bones. There was an execution tree outside our hotel. Death was too easy. One morning in our hotel I met a literary hero of mine, Okot p'bitek, a legend in African literature. He was saying some harsh things and my colleague, in a friendly way, accused him of trying to be provocative just for provocative's sake, of not being serious. Okot p'bitek called two soldiers over to our table, told them to take my friend outside and execute him. Not in a friendly way. We joked our way out of it. But life was cheap. Death was easy. I wanted out. I couldn't take anymore.

I decided one afternoon to break away from my group, walked off to the far side of a village, looking for a place to be alone, maybe cry unseen, no need to make a fool of myself. I found a quiet spot, bowed my head, tried to pray. Suddenly I felt a little hand worm its way into mine. I looked down, saw a little girl. She pointed at a mound in front of where I was standing. "That's my Daddy," she said. "He was burned alive and I had to watch."

Sometimes in life there is an emptiness that is quite filling. This was one of those times. I was completely empty. I had nothing to give her, nothing to say. No Bible verse came to mind. I didn't pat her on the head and say, "don't worry, little girl, Habitat will build you a house." I was empty.

In that emptiness I knelt down, hugged her, and cried with her.

By this still early point in my Habitat career I already believed that Habitat's greatest gift, our most distinctive feature, was love. Millard would later empower that idea, that truism, with a wonderfully titled book, *Love in the Mortar Joints*. It was popular in Habitat circles to quote the scripture, "unless the Lord builds a house, it is built in vain." We tried to make that even more intimate, more practical, more tangible, "unless love builds a house, it is built in vain." Love comes first, then the house.

In the dirt of that tortured village in northern Uganda, I tried to get at least the first part right. I kept my mouth shut and allowed God's love to pour out on both of us.

Habitat's unofficial start was in Africa, specifically Zaire, more specifically in Mbandaka where all of Millard's vision, energy, commitment to the poor, and entrepreneurial instincts came together. But Habitat's story is even more the story of people who caught Millard's *infectious Habititis,* as he called it. Habitat would be nothing without all those people who heard this crazy idea and said, "Yes, that's it, that'll work, that's what I want to give myself to."

Mompongo Mo Imana was one of those people. I met him as part of my "checking out Habitat tour." From Millard's book to Americus, Georgia, from Koinonia's first Habitat village to a Habitat Board meeting, my immersion was both quick and gradual. So far everything checked out. In 1978 I went back to Zaire on another American Baptist-sponsored mission trip. I made plans for a side trip up to the literal equator, Mbandaka, where it was possible to stand on both sides of the equator at the same time. My life was about to experience the same changing course that a bowl of water would experience if you switched it over the equator. I was there to see what Millard had set in motion on one side of the equator, and whether it could work on another side ... mine.

In Millard's first book, *Bokotola*, he told of his own life's journey that eventually landed him in Mbandaka and

Ntondo, Zaire. His drivenness, early business success, failing marriage, and faith crisis laid the foundation for conversion.

We often joked that he was the same person after conversion as before, except that after he did everything for God and the poor, whereas before he did everything for himself. With converted priorities, God took those same "Type A" qualities and put him to work on the banks of the Zaire/Congo River, administering a defunct mission project. Quickly, Millard turned an idle brick making machine into a tool for starting Habitat For Humanity worldwide. From making bricks as an employment scheme for poor Zairians, they began to put those bricks into homes for the poor, using those same people to help do the work – "sweat equity."

The idea caught on so quickly in Mbandaka that a man from the village of Ntondo asked Millard to bring Habitat there. In other words, in short order an idea born in the red clay of southwestern Georgia surrounded by pecan trees was taking root in the chaotic cities and lush forest of Zaire. Poor people, working together, helping one another, could build a simple house at a price they could afford, and get them out of the dust and dirt and mud of squalid huts.

At least Millard's book said so. He was right.

That's how I met Mompongo Mo Imana, also known as Sam.

The ruthless dictator of Zaire, Mobutu, pushed the idea of "authenticity," in opposition to anything connected to colonialism. No neckties, no western dress, no Christian names, no "Congo." So Congo became Zaire, and Sam became Mompongo.

What a man, by any name. Once he became acquainted with the Habitat idea he wanted it for his village. As Millard returned to America to formally organize Habitat For Humanity, Mompongo was about to become one of the most inspiring, exciting faces of Habitat. I would guess that for the first ten years of Habitat's existence, Mompongo was the key international figure in the Habitat world.

Humble, dignified, with a real passion for his people, Mompongo is a heartbreaking symbol of the hopes and despairs of post-colonial 20th century Africa. He was among that first group of Africans brought to America in the heady days of the 60's when we were sure that if we could immerse enough "third world students" in American universities we could change the world. Mompongo, a French-speaking Zairian with not a word of English, ended up at a university in the state of Washington and excelled. He returned to Zaire to help his people during a time filled with the promise and idealism of independence. When he met Millard, Mompongo was a rising star in the field of education, serving both state and central governments. His heart never lost sight of his hometown, Ntondo, situated right on a lake. It was a fishing village, mainly, and the hope was to do everything possible to improve the lives of the people. When it came to dreaming big dreams, Millard and Mompongo were a matched set.

When we met in 1978 I was smitten with Mompongo. Here was a great man, with all that greatness wrapped up in niceness and kindness. Like so many of the really good people attracted to HFH, he wanted to do good in the right way. Habitat was the vehicle for bringing as much goodness as he could to his area.

Being in Ntondo was to step into another world in another time. We crossed the lake in a dugout canoe, sometimes poling our way, sometimes helped by a motor. At one village people were summoned to the first organizing meeting of Habitat by the beating of drums, huge, hollowed out logs with different tones. In Ntondo, village meetings were held around a gigantic bonfire, organized by age group with the elders closest to the fire and most certain to be heard. The younger you were, the farther away you sat. Grateful villagers delivered wild boar, elk, snake and dried fish to Mompongo's door each day for our nourishment.

In many ways, Ntondo was a dry run for what HFH would soon be doing all over the developing world. Which means we made a lot of mistakes. We experimented, learned, did a lot of good. For example, we sent idealistic young volunteers to oversee the project. Millard told of sending one young adult to Zaire in the early days, and his entire training was to read Millard's *Bokotola* on the flight. Others would follow with more training as HFH departmentalized, expanding with emphases on U.S. Affiliates, Overseas Sponsored Projects, Volunteer Training and eventually even a model village exhibiting HFH houses from around the world. But that was much later.

In Ntondo we sent volunteers, purchased a big truck, started a lumber mill to provide our own wood, and entered the very real world of a very real traditional village. It was an exciting mix when we did things right and when we did things wrong.

I'll share two stories of doing things right. Outside Ntondo lived several Pygmy families, a distinctive tribe that was not only shorter in stature but in status as well. They weren't liked, and certainly not wanted except to be used as near slave labor. Yet HFH insisted on building houses for all in need, regardless of tribe or status. The people of Ntondo did not want Pygmies living next door. Period.

Habitat readily agreed that people have a right to their own prejudices. No one has to live next door to a Pygmy. It was equally true that HFH was under no obligation to build houses in Ntondo for people so picky. We packed up and made ready to leave. Suddenly, folks couldn't wait to embrace Pygmy neighbors.

On another occasion, the Ntondo worksite was undermined by the constant theft of tools. Once again we considered closing up shop, going away. Instead, someone remembered the Lord's Prayer, the part that says, "lead us not into temptation." Leaving expensive tools lying around the worksite was too much temptation for someone who could imagine getting a month's worth of food for a hungry family for the right tool. Why not just lock up the tools at night? It worked.

Some of the mistakes were of my own making as I jumped into the exuberance of changing the world. I once spent three solid days interviewing the high school students of Ntondo in preparation for finding scholarships for them all across America, just as America had once done for Mompongo. I lifted up their sights and hopes and dreams with no thought to how the world of education for foreign students had changed. Zaire, for example, was already firmly in the U.S.A. camp during the Cold War, we no longer needed to impress impressionable young minds in a country that was already signed, sealed and delivered as a reliable ally. U.S. colleges also wanted paying foreign students, the children of the rich who could pay full freight. Not the daughter of a lake fisherman who lived far away not only from electricity but also from the seat of power.

It was also hard to say "no" to Mompongo's other dreams, especially when they blended so nicely with my own. He wanted a village library. I love books. It was probably 500th on the list of needs, but our passion poured a lot of effort and money into something that was just a personal whim. And never came to be.

Mompongo had other dreams, brilliant dreams. People survive in a place like Ntondo because they know nature, respect it, use it, study it, tap into it. Millard told a story of one of his daughters having had a parasite, and a Zairian fetching a certain leaf which, when wrapped around the arm, drew the parasite out. Indigenous medicine, naturopathic, whatever it may be called today, Mompongo was onto it long ago. He wanted to plant a natural medicine garden right in the heart of Ntondo. Send the knowledgeable folks deep into the forest, gather all the healing leaves and roots and barks they have known forever, bring them to the garden, plant them, grow them right there. I don't know if it ever happened.

Sadly, by the early 90's, Mompongo was a thoroughly broken man, suffering a near total mental breakdown, unable to function, retreating into a long ago childhood. Millard used every influence to get him the best care, and made it possible for two of his children to come to America for education. Mompongo died in the early 90's but for those Habitat people who encountered him in Habitat's first ten years or so, there was no better image, no better representative of Africa or mission or Habitat. Dignified, gracious, hopeful, visionary, brilliant.

But why, ultimately, broken? It is not fair to hazard an amateur guess. But I wonder about the weight of dashed hopes, doomed dreams. He had grown up in the exciting days of independence, whisked off to America for an unparalleled advantage and opportunity, returned to serve the people. Yet year by year his nation descended deeper into an abyss. Bribery, corruption, tribalism, bloodshed, civil war, the denigration of any good thing. Maybe it all just broke his heart, and his mind went along for the ride.

Mompongo also keenly felt the scourge of colonialism, and the racism that went with it. Zaire was the old Belgian Congo, first owned privately by King Leopold before being taken over by Belgium. Congo/Zaire's eighty years of colonialism were among the most brutal in all of Africa. Maximum terror inflicted on the population, with minimum development. Anyone would have presumed that independence would be better, freer, safer, nicer, kinder. By 1990, independence wasn't delivering. The nation was fractured, broken, broke, and bloody. Mompongo knew the despair of the present, and the hopelessness of the past. That had to hurt. If he was heart-broken the tears went way back, and both uses of that word "tears" would still be true. During one HFH speaking tour Mompongo stayed with us in New York. He was a living endorsement of all we were trying to do. Audiences everywhere just naturally assumed that if Habitat was attracting people like him then we must be OK. Everywhere he went he was admired, loved, respected, embraced, believed. And he knew it.

Except at Sabena Airlines. Sabena was the national airline of Belgium, and as the former colonial power they monopolized air travel in and out of Zaire. During that New York visit, Mompongo needed to make some adjustments in his flights so we took the subway to midtown Manhattan, where Sabena Airlines had its office. Together we strode along the Manhattan sidewalks like two good friends who owned the world. Life was good, we were good.

Then Mompongo saw the Sabena Airlines sign. At that instant his proud walk turned into a painfully slow shuffle, shoulders stooped. As we approached the counter, he didn't lift his eyes, he presented his ticket without eye contact, he barely mumbled his request.

Twenty minutes later we were back on 5th Avenue eating Sabrett's hotdogs, blending in easily with all the other successful businessmen and happy tourists.

On his next visit, exactly the same thing happened. Twenty years after independence, with an amazing college degree from an outstanding American college, with power and influence and success back home, with respect and popularity following his every step, yet the degrading effects of growing up under racist colonialism could push all that far, far away. What role this played in his final break from reality I don't know. I know that it broke my heart.

I could go on, I should go on. One of the names for Africa is "the forgotten continent." Every now and then Africa suffers some horrific event and it is remembered for a day or week, then quickly recedes into forgotteness. Maybe if I write more it will keep Africa in our consciousness, or at least mine, a bit longer. A silly notion, I know.

I am reminded of the very end of the twentieth chapter of the Gospel of John. John tells the extraordinary life of Jesus, right through convincing accounts of Jesus' resurrection. Then he writes, almost off handedly, "I could tell you a lot more but enough's enough," to paraphrase. Then John adds a bit more.

I could tell you a lot more stories. Idi Amin's rebel soldiers tracking us down deep in an abandoned game reserve, pointing their machine guns and taking off the safety lock. Being held up in Kinshasa by another machine gun toting gang, who, when told that we were Christians, proudly declared, "We're Christians, too!"

But other stories, too. While my sister Donna and her husband David were serving with Habitat in Zaire, my twin nieces were delivered in a mission hospital. Born while

Donna was sick with malaria *and* hepatitis, my beloved nieces' very survival was made possible only by the combined efforts of missionary doctors and Zairian nurses and donated blood, all of which turned death into life. The stories remembered by family and friends who served with HFH in Zaire have kept Africa more remembered – stories of houses built and crises resolved and lessons learned along the way.

The best lesson was the simple reminder that it is all about people. Whether you talk about world mission, or church work, or Habitat For Humanity, it is all about people. That's the powerful lesson of Jesus' own ministry. It was all about people. Not power, not structure, not tradition, not numbers, not doctrine. People.

Donna and David taught me that when they returned from Zaire, hale and hearty, with my thriving nieces. They visited our church in Massachusetts and presented their HFH slide show. For two years they had directed our thriving Habitat project. I was president of HFH, our church was deeply involved, we gave a lot of money, we built houses ourselves, so we couldn't wait to see their visual report from the front lines.

They did their slide show. Not one house. Not one brick. Not one hammer. Just people. It was the most effective demonstration of Habitat we had ever seen. And it was all about people.

I was 28 when I first went to Africa. A young pastor, wet behind the ears, immature, ignorant in the real sense of the word. I knew nothing. Africa became my teacher. Sometimes by looking far away we can better see what is close by. For me, I learned more about being a pastor and being a Christian, about ministry and mission, about faith and works, than I ever thought possible.

In the early '8os, I began my Doctoral studies, encouraged by a great pastor who challenged me "to put knowledge to my intuition." He was impressed by my experiences and take away from all those visits to Africa. He sensed that I was learning important lessons, and he wanted me to get an academic, scholarly, accredited seal of approval for what I was getting in my gut. I did that, it was a lot of fun, rigorous, rewarding. But the truth is I had already been schooled, walking in Millard's footsteps near the Zaire River, trying to match the passion of Mompongo, drinking palm wine deep in the bush with Gene Gentry and Mankwela, re-learning the Bible through the eyes of the widows in Uganda, understanding what real faith was all about. Whatever else I have accomplished as a pastor, or with Habitat, or in the world of mission, it all began in Africa.

Chapter Seven
Nicaragua

Habitat took me to lots of places. But I've often said that if I could only revisit one place it would be Nicaragua.

I loved everything from the people to the topography, from the coffee to the cigars, from the challenges to the opportunities.

And the worst housing situation I've ever seen was in Nicaragua. More about that later.

Before I ever got to Nicaragua I got immersed in a tiny bit of U.S./Nicaraguan politics. In the fall of 1984, Daniel Ortega , the newly-elected President of Nicaragua, came to New York City to speak at The United Nations. He decided he wanted to visit the HFH project on the Lower East Side of Manhattan, a project made famous by one of Jimmy Carter's first Work Camps.

Ortega was the former revolutionary who led the Sandinista rebels in the overthrow of the U.S. backed Samoza dictatorship. The U.S. and Ortega have been at each other's throats for decades, to this day.

Conscious of public opinion and the effect of politics on fundraising, HFH was concerned about a high-profile visit from an avowed Communist Latin American revolutionary to an equally high profile Habitat project.

For me, the issue was simple. We had just recently voted to begin Habitat work in Nicaragua. That would mean U.S. dollars, Habitat volunteers, U.S. citizens in work camps, and Habitat staff hoping to be in and out of Nicaragua, unimpeded, even helped by that government. If we were expecting such help, how could we tell the head of their government that he couldn't even see us in action right here in America?

And one more thing. Why would we ever turn down the opportunity to present the Good News in a living way ... to anyone, including a Latin American revolutionary?!!

So, before I knew it, there I was in a hotel room across from the UN, sitting with Daniel Ortega, his wife and family, and their fellow revolutionaries. Then down the elevator into a police-escorted motorcade through midtown Manhattan, all the way to East 6th Street and Avenue C, "Alphabet City."

For me, it was all "upside." Ortega got to see Habitat in action, the Gospel in action, "the word made flesh," a Christianity that is talked and taught and done. Sweat-equity homeowners, the beginnings of a revitalized neighborhood, the "theology of the hammer," all on display.

The pay-off? Who knows! I do know that Habitat took root in Nicaragua and I had a few chances to see it firsthand. From the late 1980s to 1991 I had three visits there.

The first was actually not Habitat-related. It was more of a fact finding trip put together by peace activists known to one another through Habitat. Don Mosley organized the trip. Probably no one had a more tangled history with Millard and Habitat than Don. He had been at Koinonia with the Fullers even before there was a Habitat, and he helped get HFH up and running in Zaire. He was a longtime member of HFH's Board of Directors, which meant that we worked side by side for more than ten years. Truth be told, Don was Millard's staunchest defender, right through the final sexual harassment charges that finally were Millard's undoing in 2005.

In the 1980s Don began a new Christian community called Jubilee Partners in Comer, Georgia. With his unwavering commitment to peace, the very hot/cold war of Nicaragua was on his heart. The U.S./Soviet cold war was played out by the Contras'/Sandinistas' hot war. U.S. involvement was obvious and deadly, and, whether realistic or not, people actually imagined an upcoming U.S. military invasion of Nicaragua. Nicaraguans feared it, and there were Americans who wanted it. This was the political backdrop to our visit.

The trip felt like the movie, *Casablanca,* re-set in Central America. Slow-moving overhead fans, hot and humid air, spies, soldiers, tension. I kept hoping Lauren Bacall would show up.

We began the trip in Tegucigalpa, the capital of Honduras, the staging ground of the American-backed Contras. As soon as I stepped off the plane, I remember feeling like everyone was listening in on our conversations. The paranoia had been building for weeks. In the weeks leading up to our trip, Don and I often talked on the phone, and signs of wiretapping were so obvious that we sometimes talked to our unknown third party. The joke seemed less funny once we hit Central America. About ten days later, after our Nicaraguan visit was completed, I returned to Tegucigalpa alone and it was even scarier. I remember buying my son a beautifully engraved machete, and carrying it around with the handle half out so that my imaginary assassins would think twice.

On the way to Nicaragua, we stopped over in El Salvador, just days after a devastating earthquake. El Salvador was suffering its own bloody civil war so we never got out of the capital city, San Salvador. We zeroed in on the earthquake damage and relief efforts. We saw the sacrifice of so many American donors who funded the vital work of Americares, The Red Cross, and the many missionaries who were hard at work. I visited one Baptist church, associated with my American Baptist denomination, filled to the rafters with foodstuffs funded by our churches. Seeing families come in to the church, people who lost everything, and then go home with baskets laden with food, knowing that only the week before some folks in Iowa or Massachusetts had put a little extra in the offering plate for El Salvador, that was good.

But Nicaragua was our destination. Maybe it was more like a Graham Greene novel. Exotic. Intrigue. More tension. More spies. The country was now run by overtly communist revolutionaries, the Sandinistas, who had driven out a long time dictator, Samoza. So the air was a mixture of euphoria along with that intrigue and tension. The Bible says, "the old has passed, the new has come," but no one quite knew what the new would bring. Our various visits and meetings bore that out.

One day we went to the Roman Catholic Cardinal's head-quarters. Our goal was to encourage the Cardinal to be a more even-handed arbiter of peace between the U.S. backed Contras and the now-in-power Sandinistas. The Cardinal was clearly anti-Sandinista and pro-Contra. At the meeting, when we asked church authorities to use their influence to bring the Contras to the peace table, there was a telling response. We were told, "if a father has two children who are fighting you don't grab just one, you wait for the right moment when you get both." My immediate thought was, "spoken like someone with no kids! If you have two kids fighting, you actually grab the first one you can and sit them down!!"

Actually, the role of religion in Nicaragua was quite interesting. Before going there I was interviewed on a radio station in New York City, and the guest before me was talking about the oppression of churches in Nicaragua. Churches were locked, and there was no Sunday morning worship anywhere, the guest proclaimed.

Not exactly true. I remember a couple of towns I visited. It was true, some of the churches did not have Sunday morning services. They had services seven nights a week! One Sunday evening we attended Catholic Mass in Managua, the capital city. The church was packed. Whatever else the Sandinistas were up to, they weren't weakening Christianity.

A more interesting meeting took place at the offices of the main newspaper, La Prensa, which happened to be an opposition paper. Violeta Chamorro was the publisher, and head of a very divided family. One son edited La Prensa, another edited the Sandinista paper. At La Prensa, one editor appealed for American intervention to overthrow the Sandinistas and bring the Contras, and his paper, to power. He was quite passionate about it.

I asked him what would happen if U.S. soldiers did invade Nicaragua. "They will win the cities and lose the mountains," he responded. "And it will be a long war it cannot win." But he still wanted it.

The most difficult part of my Nicaraguan journey was pure serendipity. Early in our trip a truckload of Nicaraguan *campesinos*, farmers, were blown to pieces by landmines planted by the Contras. My American tax dollars at work.

Three of us made the decision to leave the main group and drive into the mountains where a makeshift field hospital was caring for the wounded. Our trip led to the stupidest question I have ever asked. Given that we were on the way to visit the battered survivors of a landmine explosion in the middle of a road, our drive was tension-packed. So I asked our driver, "How do you know when it's a landmine?"

"It goes 'boom.'"

I told you it was a stupid question.

But nothing prepared me for the hospital visit. The truck load of campesinos was made up of a Christian pastor, and many of his church members and fellow villagers, on their way to market in a neighboring town. Blown up by bombs I paid for, planted by soldiers paid for by me and Ollie North. That afternoon I personally visited a dozen victims, some with amputations, all badly wounded. One day they are blown up by American dollars at work, the next day an American is sitting on their cot. And I did not hear a single word of bitterness, anger, anti-Americanism or revenge. "Pray for us, and work for peace," the pastor told me.

I learned a valuable lesson in Nicaragua. It had been dawning on me for years as I went to Africa, India, Haiti, Peru, but in the mountains of Nicaragua it became clear. One man said to me, "all we want is S and S."

I replied, "S and S?"– not getting it.

"Staple and Security," he explained. And literally in that moment I remembered all the experiences I had had among the poor and oppressed and targeted. They all just wanted "S and S – staple and security." The right to travel from one village to the next without being killed just because. Just because they are the wrong religion, wrong tribe, wrong color, wrong answer, or wrong time. And every people on earth has its own staple food: banana in Uganda, rice in India, potato in Peru, corn and beans in Nicaragua, manioc in Zaire. Pretty simple: staple and security. That's all the pastor in the mountains of Nicaragua wanted for his people. A little corn, and no "boom."

I had another revelation there. My denomination, the American Baptist Churches USA, was very involved in missionary work in Nicaragua, pouring money and people into noble ministries among the poor. It struck me as counterintuitive, and counter-productive. I actually wrote a tongue-in-cheek letter to my denomination and used a similar message in speaking engagements when I returned home. My message was this: we should either use our mission dollars to fund the Contra rebels and stop the missionary work; or we should work hard to stop funding the Contras. It seemed silly to try to get Nicaraguans baptized and blown up. One or the other.

I made similar comments at an early morning peace vigil outside the U.S. Embassy in Managua. My original motivation for going to Nicaragua, and the reason my church allowed me the time to go, was to see the situation and develop an informed opinion before American blood started to be shed. As we have often seen, once U.S. soldiers are sent to war and begin to die nobody wants to hear "a discouraging word" or negative comment. We are more open-minded before our blood starts to flow. That is why I was in Nicaragua at that moment. Once there, what I saw and heard convinced me to do everything I could to encourage the Nicaraguan people, and nothing to divide them; and to do everything I could to keep the United States from adding fuel to the fire. In other words, to get the Cardinal's two "children" to sit down and stop fighting.

Habitat was my main focus on my visits and provided some great experiences. Even our little fact-finding group spent a day building houses in a rural village. I'm not sure I'll ever be invited back. My brick-laying partner and I were so immersed in conversation that the house wall we built had to be de-constructed the next day.

That night I had a face-to-face encounter with a snake. We were put up in people's homes in the village. Mine was a sort of stick and wattle house, two rooms, dirt floor. I woke up at three a.m., turned over and met the snake. Over the years, the snake has gotten larger and larger in my re-telling, which is unnecessary since it was big enough already.

In previous Habitat trips to places with scary animals I had adopted a "live and let live" policy based on friendly conversation with whatever was scaring me to death. This worked with spiders in Zaire, pythons and baboons in Uganda, and an embarrassing encounter with a cobra in India – that turned out to be a bullfrog. My policy was based on wisdom given to me by an early Habitat volunteer who met (and survived) a lonely face-to-face with a gorilla. "Don't run," he told me, "stay put, and talk nice, you might live."

So I began to talk to the snake. Kind words. Soft words. Words of encouragement. I asked about his family. Told him about mine. Reminded him of why I was in his village. Yes, his village, I made that very clear. And I promised that as soon as the sun came up I was leaving. The rest of the night passed slowly.

The next day, because of my love for baseball, I was taken to meet an elderly man who was a baseball legend in the area. He was lying in his hammock and glad to meet another old baseball player, especially a catcher, since he was an outstanding pitcher. I noticed his very crooked arm, bent badly at the elbow, and asked about it. He laughed, "I got that throwing hand grenades at the Yanquis." Later on, in one of those 1980s movies set in Central American revolutions, there was a scene of a renowned pitcher throwing hand grenades. Life imitating art, or the other way around – I don't know.

On another visit I met two Nicaraguan baseball teams leaving our hotel for a game in a particularly volatile area. They weren't worried, they assured me, and even I should feel safe in coming to the game because neither side, Contras nor Sandinistas, would disrupt a baseball game. I couldn't decide if that was comforting or disturbing.

I often wondered how I was perceived, traveling about. One night I was brought to a huge theatre to introduce the idea of Habitat to a packed house. Do you believe in "speaking in tongues," the idea that God gives you language to express what you might otherwise not be able to express? That night there was no translator available, so calling upon my high school Spanish from decades earlier I preached for an hour, entirely in the present tense. I asked my host how I did. "Terrific!" he said, "Putting everything in the present tense gave the whole message a sense of immediacy."

Afterward a few of us went to a little bar/café. Seated at the next table was a particularly fierce-looking fellow, with a big pistol tucked into his belt.

"Are you a communist?" he growled at me in Spanish. I managed a very weak-voiced "no."

"Then you must be a Christian. Only communists and Christians come up here to help."

"Si, soy un Cristiano, un evangelico," I said, using the word for Protestant, thinking that he didn't look like a fan of the Cardinal's.

My final memory lives with me every day as I am a true coffee lover. With Habitat I've seen the most abysmal housing conditions imaginable. World famous slums in Calcutta and Bombay/Mumbai, a literal cesspool neighborhood in Cap Haïtien, Haiti, squatters and card-board condominiums in New York City.

But the worst was a couple of hours outside Managua on a coffee plantation. The coffee pickers were housed in a sort of dormitory or barn. It was cut up into the tiniest possible "apartments." Perhaps six feet long at best, maybe six feet high, four or five feet wide. For an entire family, everybody on one bed. All so I could have a cheap cup of coffee.

As I sit writing this chapter in my local coffeehouse, the news of the day features a Christian militia group in Michigan preparing for war against our government as part of their "end times" theology. Their definition of The Gospel, evidently, is to provoke an incident that would lead to killing police or soldiers, which would elicit a bloody response that would lead to greater bloodshed.

I will always be proud that Habitat-type folks find the Gospel compelling them to form into groups that practice Love. And I just hope that a couple of those groups found their way to that coffee plantation.

Chapter Eight
India

I had no interest in India. Zero. Nada. But I learned more about Habitat there, and about mission, than anywhere else. By 1983 I was finishing my Doctorate with a thesis focused on mission and Africa. That May I began an exciting challenge as a pastor moving from New York to Massachusetts. Habitat was growing by leaps and bounds.

My plate was full.

Onto that full plate stepped Dr. David Purushothaman, a humble Indian immigrant pastor in New Jersey. Humble and persistent. And more than anything he wanted Habitat in India. For that to happen he needed to get me to India.

To that point HFH was a mostly African, somewhat Latin American, and rural U.S. ministry. Asia was new and unknown to us. At that time India was not in the sphere of western influence. Although a leader in the "Non-Aligned Movement" of nations, India was cozier with the old Soviet Union than with the United States. In other words, I had no idea what I was headed into.

I was headed into the most dramatic confrontation with God I have ever had. But I'm getting ahead of myself.

Dr. David took me to India to find the best place to start a HFH project, our first in Asia. We had a whirlwind visit with two dynamic Bishops as our hosts. The Church of South India was the world's first ecumenical denomination, created out of the euphoria of India's independence and post-World War II, bringing together several denominations. In the state of Tamil Nadu Bishop Sam Ponniah of Vellore and Bishop Sundar Clark of Madras (now renamed Chennai) introduced us to a world of hurt—drought, grinding poverty, over-whelming need. Yet the Good News of Jesus Christ prospered. In the most remote villages and in the teeming streets of big cities people found hope in Christ. Nobody was giving up.

David Purushothaman was the grandson of a Hindu priest who chose to believe in Jesus Christ as God's redeem-ing son. His grandmother was killed and the rest of the fam-ily barely escaped with their lives when their village erupted against their choice of Christ. David grew up, became a pas-tor, and taught me a lot about patience, perseverance, cour-age. One story teaches a lot. David, as a young pastor, went out to the rural villages to share the Good News. These could be arduous as well as dangerous visits. Twice he was bitten by scorpions at night while sleeping in a remote area. On one occasion he was invited into the humble home of a villager. Before he could speak, before the villager would listen, the man went over to the side of the room, lifted the cover off a jar, scooped a cup of room temperature milk, and placed it in front of David. It was filled with flies.

The message was clear, if unstated. You want to tell me about Jesus? You say God loves even me? God cares about my life? God has the hairs of my head numbered? You want me to listen to you? Believe you? You have "good news" for my life? Then share my life. My poverty. My sickness. My humiliation. My milk. Be one with me.

David drank the milk. The villager listened to the Gospel, and welcomed Christ into his life.

I learned a lot from the Bishops, too. Both men led by example with a genuine commitment to the poor. Bishop Ponniah's motto was "every Bishop a pastor, every pastor an evangelist." Ponniah lived his motto. He was not content to stay within the comfort of the Bishop's fine residence. We spent hours and hours driving dusty miles to god forsaken villages to make it clear – they were *NOT* God forsaken. Ponniah went as an evangelist, a bearer of good news; he went as a pastor, to care. He didn't go as a Bishop to exert authority or to enjoy adulation. He went to serve. To see, to listen, and then to bring the healing touch of God's love. At one village we arrived just hours after the entire village had burned to the ground. One thatched roof hut had caught fire, and the flames leapt from thatch to thatch. So we settled in for the day, they became our schedule, our agenda. We stayed until their tears turned to laughter, their sorrow to rejoicing.

The custom of Habitat in those days was to establish a sponsored project overseas, send American volunteers to start it, and provide the funds for building. But missionary activity was illegal in India; foreign missionaries, of any kind or purpose, were not welcome, and foreign funds were suspect. One night over dinner I asked Bishop Ponniah what he thought about American dollars and American volunteers coming to India. He gave an astounding answer: "There is no such thing as American dollars or Indian dollars. They are all God's dollars. And if it so happens that there are more of God's dollars in America than in India, then that is your problem, isn't it? And you need to figure out how to get some of God's dollars from your country to this country without causing offense, or creating dependence. And the same for volunteers. They are not American volunteers, they are God's."

This may seem obvious. But in the late twentieth century, with cross cultural mission and evangelism under attack, Ponniah's perspective was refreshing and liberating.

But that was nothing compared to what God did to me at the Bishops' houses.

At Ponniah's house in Vellore, God bestirred my soul. I mean that, God shook me to the core. To be specific, God spoke to me...with specifics. Late at night but clear as day God told me to "start a ministry, call it Friends of Christ in India, which comes out as FOCI. FOCI is the Latin plural of focus, because you are to have two *foci*, evangelism and social action. Evangelism is telling people about Jesus, and social action is doing what Jesus told us to do. FOCI is to do both. And don't take a penny for yourself." Yes, those are real quotation marks.

This was definitely not my plan. I had no time. And no idea of how to do what I was being commanded, "called," to do.

The answer came quickly. By then I was living at Bishop Clark's house in Madras, continuing a rigorous schedule of village visits, speeches, meetings and encounters. I was exhausted, emotionally and physically. I was ready to go home.

At my lowest ebb, the doorbell rang at the Bishop's house. The doorbell ringer was a short fellow, 50ish, looking and sounding like an Indian who had once studied at Cambridge and returned, and he was.

Korabandi Azariah was an evangelist from the next state, Andhra Pradesh. A product of a persistent Christian mother, he was dedicated to God's service as a child and grew into it as a man. Teaming with an equally dynamic woman, Mary Seethamma, with her own dramatic conversion story, they formed a partnership in evangelism that rivaled the best of St. Paul and Mother Teresa. No exaggeration. I am a great admirer of Mother Teresa and visited much of her work, and it is a compliment to both to put them in the same sentence.

But I didn't know this that Sunday afternoon in Madras. I had just preached at majestic St. George's Cathedral, I had just finished an amazing and overwhelming couple of weeks laying the groundwork for Habitat in Asia, God had spoken to me, and so I was quite full of myself. I felt very well used and much honored, and done. I was ready to go home.

Did I mention another of God's little coincidences? Azariah had been working alongside Mary Seethamma since the 50's. Mary Seethamma had relatives who immigrated to New Jersey. The relatives rented an apartment from David Purushothaman. When David forced me to go to India, the relatives forced us to agree to meet Azariah.

Frankly, Azariah had no desire to meet me. He had been praying for months to attend a once in a lifetime Billy Graham conference in Amsterdam specifically for itinerant evangelists—which he was, first and foremost. An itinerant evangelist is a modern day Apostle Paul, going from place to place to tell about Jesus. No job, no security, no income, no marriage, no support system. Yet, Azariah was rejected by the conference, and it bothered him. He wasn't in a good mood.

He was stuck in a really out of the way town in the next state. I did not want to see another dusty town, another empty well, another leper, another million emaciated beggars, another church full of happy people, despite it all.

Nevertheless, we hopped on the train to Khammam, a mere ten hour trip. He forgot to mention that.

Once there God completed upturning my life. In Azariah and his team I met people who totally fulfilled the midnight call from God to start FOCI and to pay attention both to "evangelism" and "social action." These folks surely talked about Jesus, but they also walked the talk. For three decades they had patiently and lovingly served the poor, with no backing, no structure behind them. By the sweat of their brow they just did what Azariah called "the needful." Whatever it took. "See a need, meet a need," he told me, explaining his priorities.

If ever someone was tailor-made for Habitat it was Azariah. Especially back in those days when HFH was so young we needed leaders with vision. We weren't a household name even in the U.S.A. Therefore we needed leaders able to imagine the houses, the families, the impact, the benefits, and the way forward. We also needed leaders with a thorough commitment to the poor, with a mature devotion to God in Christ, and with the experience to work within the system of their own country. Azariah was all of that. He had a lifetime of experience, a proven track record, an unmitigated zeal to serve, a willingness to get his own hands dirty.

By the time I returned to America I had a proposal for the first HFH project in all of Asia. Today that one project has built over two thousand houses, and it has spread throughout India, north and south, and across Asia.

And, God called my bluff. Suddenly I had the place, the people, and the opportunity to start FOCI. With Millard's blessing, and even contributions, I started FOCI in order to raise funds to help Azariah do what he was already doing, and more of what he was doing, and to get around to doing some of the things he always wanted to do.

Today FOCI has schools, medical work, youth hostels, feeding centers, churches, evangelism, homes for the aged and lots more. Social action and evangelism beautifully wedded together. But that's another story. (For a sense of *that* story, information about FOCI is listed at the end of this book.)

The important thing is that God knew what to do, where to do it, who to do it with. The end result is that Habitat and FOCI took root together, prospered, and have been a blessing to hundreds of thousands of people.

I learned a lot along the way.

Habitat took off splendidly in Khammam, and two years later exactly I was back there to dedicate the first HFH houses, and the first FOCI project, a church. They both met challenges unique to India in creative and loving ways.

When I first met with the HFH organizing folks in 1983 I spoke to them about "the Gospel as a surprise." It was common for missionary activity to benefit Christians. Even when it wasn't the intention it was the perception. With HFH providing such a valuable commodity, a house, the temptation at every HFH project in every country was to benefit one's own—one's own tribe, clan, family, religion, church, caste, denomination. I remember saying in Khammam, "If Christians in America send money to Christians in India to build houses for poor Christians, there's no surprise in that. But if Christians in America send money to Christians in India to build houses for those most in need, even for someone in a caste that has historically looked down on you, or a caste that you looked down upon, or from a religion that has persecuted you, that is a surprise. So let the Gospel be a surprise."

It worked better than I hoped. When I was back there to dedicate the first batch of twenty-two houses, we kept the Habitat tradition of giving every new homeowner a Bible, so we did. That next Sunday I preached at St. Mary's Church in Khammam. Seated right on the floor in front of the pulpit were those twenty-two families, mostly Hindu. What were they doing there? They had their house, they didn't need to ingratiate themselves to me. One homeowner put it simply.

"We saw what you do. Now we want to read your book." The Gospel was a surprise.

The surprise only multiplied. When we dedicated our first FOCI church in the village of Janikapuram, it was another grand celebration. It is their custom to do all the formal ceremony outside a new church. Then, when all the preaching, singing, praying is done there is an elaborate ribbon cutting and very formal unlocking of the door. The only door. The only entrance. Remember that.

In my sermon outside I emphasized that I hoped that the church would always be a place for all people in the village, Hindu, Muslim, Christian. This village had become our first ever FOCI project because they, too, called my bluff. Two years earlier I had challenged them. They had asked me for a church. I told them bluntly that if they sent me a list of every villager and their contribution to building a church, and if they dug the foundation and got some work done, then I would find the money for their church.

A few months later I got a fat envelope with a list of all the contributors and contributions—money, chickens, rice, grains. And photos of everybody digging the foundation.

My little sermon at the church dedication picked up on that theme, expressing Jesus' requirement that God's house should be a house of prayer for all people.

Then we cut the ribbon, unlocked the only door, walked in, and there was a Hindu man, an elderly farmer, standing before the cross, hands together and uplifted, offering a prayer. How did he get in? How long had he been there? You know, I never thought to ask. I was so overwhelmed that I just accepted it, miracle or not.

I could tell a hundred great FOCI stories because once Habitat kicked me out the door my India life was, is, FOCI.

But for eight years my Habitat and FOCI lives were quite intertwined. This isn't a FOCI book. It is enough for now to give thanks that Habitat provided the opportunity for me to meet the people I met and to do the work we do. It has only taken twenty years for me to be able to say that.

One of the best compliments that Azariah received was meant as a criticism. When I joined the HFH staff there was a man in my department who just couldn't stand Azariah. Or maybe he couldn't stand me and just took it out on Azariah. But he consistently did everything in his power to denigrate Azariah and his Habitat project. On one conference call to India he threatened to end funding for Khammam HFH. This guy didn't know what to do with Azariah's response, "That is all right. You can keep the money. You should do what you must do. We will keep doing what God gives us the opportunity to do."

One of that man's complaints against Azariah was that the Khammam HFH houses looked too small, too measly, not like good houses. Actually, I used that as my measuring stick for HFH houses, telling people all over that when you build a house that is embarrassingly too small for a family that can barely afford the payments, then you are doing it right. The intersection of a simple decent house with a simple decent family is where the power of the cross shows so clearly in Habitat.

Millard knew that we would always have to fight against creeping extravagance in HFH projects, stateside or overseas. Well-meaning people always wanted us to do more, provide more, build more, nicer, fancier, larger. But the HFH goal was to get as poor a family as possible into as good a house as possible that they could have the pride in paying for.

Azariah was the perfect partner for HFH and for Millard. With their "can do" spirit, anything seemed possible. There were two early crises that showed Azariah, Millard and Habitat at their best.

In those days, the 1980s, HFH insisted on each overseas "sponsored" project being led by one of Habitat's "international partners." That would be some person or couple, trained in Americus in all the Habitat whys and wherefores, the HFH way. Somebody had to translate Americus, Georgia style Habitat into Latin American, African, and now Indian reality.

But India didn't allow missionaries of any kind, by any name. For them, missionaries or "international partners" smacked of colonialism, paternalism, mistrust.

Time for a God's coincidence. Jimmy Carter's mother, Lillian, had served in India as a Peace Corps volunteer. A lovely, nostalgic letter from the former President of the United States to the Prime Minister of India opened a closed door. Our International Partners were admitted.

House payments were also critical to a successful HFH. Habitat wasn't a give-away project. We had been sternly warned that HFH would not work in India, that people simply would not make their payments. It wasn't long before we had our first family falling behind with their payment. The too small house had found a too poor family.

What are the options? Kick her out. Look the other way. Find a benefactor to pay her payment.

Or, "see a need, meet a need."

The delinquent homeowner was a widow with children in her care. In fact, the little HFH community was fairly bursting with kids. People were clamoring for some kind of schooling, but there was no money to build a school. Okay. What if, Azariah wondered, what if the widow turned her too small house into a too small school during the daytime, and the nearby families paid just enough to make her house payments? Deal done. Need seen. Need met.

Today there is a thriving school in that very first Indian Habitat neighborhood. Creative financing. Creative problem solving. Creative Habitat. Creative mission. Very Millard. Very Azariah.

One of my favorite parts of Habitat was known as Global Village. These were short term mission work camps, built around a two or three week visit to some international HFH project. I did a test run taking thirty or so people to the very high mountains of Peru, including my family. Aaron was ten at the time, Camaron was fourteen, and they had a blast. Breathing the thin, cold air of thirteen thousand feet, eating potatoes for breakfast, lunch and dinner, gobbling chocolate all day to ward off altitude sickness, trying to ignore night time bomb blasts by the Shining Path terrorist group, visiting the floating reed islands of Lake Titicaca and the ruins of Maccu Piccu, and mixing mortar and laying brick and building houses, all convinced me that HFH work camps overseas were an inspired idea.

I went on to do four Global Village work camps in India. Each one was a real immersion in Indian life, culture, religion, plus hard work. Azariah and his team programmed it all. We dug foundations, moved rocks with crowbars, mixed cement, carried bricks, and poured roofs. In the evenings we had sitar music, classical Indian dance, Bollywood movies. On Sundays we would caravan to remote villages, taking part in church services from 8 a.m. until way past midnight. And we ate whatever was put on the banana leaf in front of us.

What is the best part of these overseas, short-term mission trips? Done right, they are really humbling. I would go so far as to say that if you are not humbled by the experience then it was not a worthwhile experience. If you think you're hot stuff, superior, God's gift to the poor, and come back thinking the same way, you have just wasted two weeks and all that money.

I heard a great Mennonite missionary at the Overseas Ministries Study Center challenge us "to move to where we are uncomfortable." A good overseas mission work camp should do that. A good work camper will want that.

How does that happen? Interaction. Openness. You go with a heart to serve, a desire to learn, a willingness to try. You don't sneer at the food. You don't mock their religion. You don't romanticize or judge their poverty. You are there to love and to be loved.

One of my work camps was going just fine. We were digging and carrying and sweating, clearly helping the poor and doing good and having a ball. During our lunch break, Azariah brought by a group of lepers. They were living under a bridge, he said. The government had built them some houses, but they were so poorly constructed that they were falling in on the inhabitants. They escaped to the bridge for shelter. Later we were driven by their bridge village, and their abandoned, falling-down mini-houses. "All right, back to work" was my thought. It made for an interesting lunch break, sure, a troubling sociological problem for somebody in India to deal with. But not us. We had our Habitat work to do. We were at a new frontier in Christian mission. We were changing the world one brick at a time, one house at a time, one family at a time. We had our system down pat. Sweat equity. House payments. Enough said. Back to work.

Nobody moved. My Global Village HFH work campers refused to work. They wanted to know how I, President of Habitat for Humanity, building houses all over the world, could just look at forty families living under a bridge and not do something?! I tried talking about the importance of sweat equity, the pride that comes with building your own home. I tried to gently point out that people with Hansen's Disease (the modern term for Biblical leprosy) generally didn't have fingers and toes, for those were eaten away by their own disease. As the disease advances they are not only social outcasts, they can't do much. That's why lepers are mostly beggars. So our under-the-bridge-dwelling new friends could not do their sweat equity or make their house payments. Zero for two. The two pillars of Habitat success were beyond their capability.

"Okay?" I said. "Now, back to work."

Again, no one moved. We were all seated in one room in a no-star hotel in downtown Khammam, it was mid-afternoon – and I had a work stoppage going on. My daughter refused to budge. My friends refused to budge. My church members refused to budge. "See a need, meet a need, remember?" they seemed to be throwing at me.

Quickly we formed a plan. Khammam Habitat would write a proposal. FOCI would raise the funds. The lepers' sweat equity would be their prayers. Prayer is work, right? Takes effort, concentration, and commitment. They prayed, we did raise the funds, Habitat approved the project, Khammam people built it, Millard went over to dedicate it. Today, it is a village of three hundred people. The houses have been repaired and improved, new families added, care provided in many ways. All thanks to the stubbornness of Habitat folks. Stubbornness -- or perhaps vision.

Is there one image that captures my almost thirty years of India visits? There are too many, many too personal. My daughter's wedding in Hyderabad, with Camaron and Narendra buried under a mountain of rose petals. My grandchildren accompanying me to all of our FOCI projects, speaking to our partners and beneficiaries in their language. My son working side by side with American and Indian doctors at our old mission hospital during a free surgical camp. Camaron putting her decades of wisdom and experience to work in behalf of our projects. Seeing the kids at our FOCI schools grow up, succeed, prosper, and give back. Aaron and Camaron working with me, side by side, hand in hand.

But just one story? Okay. One story. During one of our HFH Global Village work camps, I was introduced to an Indian doctor, an obstetrician/gynecologist with her own hospital. She had a severely mentally handicapped adult son, and she wanted us to start a facility, a ministry, for him and other mentally handicapped children and young adults. Our whole HFH work team was invited to her home for lunch, and presented with gifts. The next day she held a huge public gathering, press and politicians, garlands and praise all around, to announce that FOCI had promised to build a Center for Mentally Handicapped Children. I had said no such thing. I was actually opposed to it. Not to mention that I didn't have money for it. In short, she was the most obnoxious, pushy, brassy, manipulative person I had ever met.

But she was also right. Like Millard, she had a vision based on justice. And nothing, or no one, was going to stop it.

I eventually swallowed my ego, saw the light, and set out to raise the funds. Two years later I sat on the platform for the dedication of Dr. Vasanthamma's dream come true. A middle-aged father came up to the microphone carrying his five-year-old daughter. He told us of how, when she was born, he thought it was best to do away with her. He was going to stuff her nostrils with rice, ease her into her next life. Then he looked at me. "Because of this place I am so proud to have my daughter." A few years later he told us, "She is the apple of my eye."

I have always felt, from my earliest days with HFH, that when the history of Habitat is written the actual houses may be the least important part of the story. Way above the brick and mortar will be the people, the relationships, the volunteers, the homeowners, the "aha" moments. The walls broken down may be more impressive than the best walls put up.

That happens because of the kind of serendipity that Habitat just naturally engenders or allows. HFH is the vehicle, the excuse, which brings an extraordinary array of people together in the unlikeliest combinations in the unlikeliest settings. Because of HFH, people put themselves in positions where unexpected miracles can happen. I got Habitat started in India. People wanted to go to India to help build. On a free afternoon we meet a half-crazed doctor frightened for her son's future. We get bulldozed into helping. A little girl, almost killed at birth by her father, is now his pride and joy. Serendipity. God's coincidences. The Holy Spirit at work. Whatever.

Chapter Nine
The U.S. of A.

I've already written that before I got involved in Mission I had never been farther away than New Jersey. That's not much of an exaggeration. Mentally, culturally, and for the most part physically, I've said that I was like the New Yorker Magazine cover that depicts New York City prominently and the rest of the country blurred into the unimportant world out there.

Habitat changed that.

As HFH grew, I got to see what Pete Seeger was singing about in *This Land is Your Land*. I got to see the depth and breadth, the incredible variety, the joyous peculiarities, the history, the churches, the people. And the poverty.

Habitat Headquarters began each day with devotions, a morning worship service with praise and prayer and preaching. For me the very special moment was when we would lift up in prayer a specific project, often one overseas and one stateside, and specific people from the larger HFH family.

Very often there would be a "road trip" report. In the early days it was mostly Millard reporting from a recent visit to a project or speaking engagement at some church. As years went by more and more HFH staff hit the road to expand the work, raise the funds, encourage the partners, share the hope of Habitat.

I always loved hearing those "trip reports." Each report was affirmation of what we were doing. After all, we went where we were invited. So, by definition, every trip report was proof that somebody understood what we were doing;

somebody believed that Habitat worked, somebody shared our vision and our compassion and our plan. It was proof that we weren't crazy, and we weren't alone.

My life with Habitat could easily read like one long trip report.

Habitat was my ticket to the world, but also my introduction to America. All those HFH speaking engagements and meetings took me into my own country's nooks and crannies, moving me beyond my New England roots and the northeast corridor.

I read a book about a young post-graduate student who hops into his beaten up old car and sets out across America looking for places of faith, religiosity, and spirituality. He looked for neon crosses and store-front churches and snappy outdoor bulletin boards and coffee shop flyers for all sorts of spiritual activities.

Mine was a similar journey except that my road signs and ports of call and religious landmarks were Habitat-related. I would drive into a town or fly into an airport, be met by enthusiastic HFH volunteers or search out some Habitat active church. Over the course of one, two or three days, I would do whatever I could to promote and to encourage the local Habitat project and people. Radio interviews, fund-raising banquets, house dedications, newspaper photos, visits with donors and church mission boards, tours of the streets and neighborhoods yearning for a touch of Habitat, all of this was my own little tour of America.

Those years of countless visits seem like postcards to me now, bucolic snapshot memories of good people doing good things with other good people. What was surprising and inspiring was the ordinariness of it all. There was no holier-than-thou self-righteousness, no melodrama or hype, no sense of self-importance or "look at us!! See how great we are!!!" Just neighbors being neighborly. Just Christians being Christian. Doing the right thing. Helping to build a simple, decent house for a tiny part of God's people in need. No big deal. I liked that.

These visits kept me in touch with the real Habitat. On the presidential, board, staff, headquarters level where I spent so much time, it was easy to get caught up in corporate life, mass mailings, fundraising, internal strife, big numbers, public relations, marketing, hiring/firing.

But up in Burlington, Vermont, or rural Michigan or Covington, Louisiana, or Dorchester, Massachusetts, or Jersey City, New Jersey, or Lancaster, Pennsylvania, or Lynn and Worcester and New Haven and San Antonio and San Diego and some place in Utah and another place in Florida and some other place in New Hampshire – all those postcard memories of Saturday volunteers cutting boards, pounding nails, laying sheet rock cheek to jowl with the future homeowner doing their sweat equity, those fueled my faith that faith in Habitat was good faith.

I am pretty sure it was Burlington, but it could have been any of those New England towns I love so much, where our Habitat house was part of a small housing development, perhaps twenty or twenty-five houses all told. The local authorities had set aside a few of the houses for low-income housing. Along with the lot given to Habitat to build on, another had been entrusted to the nearby Vocational/Technical High School, and the rest were being developed by professionals. The beauty of it was that you couldn't tell who built what. The high school Vo/Tech students' house and the all-volunteer Habitat house and the pro-builders' houses all looked fine, each built with pride and dedication.

This was one of Habitat's great teachings: that housing for poor people doesn't have to be poorly done, poorly designed, and poorly kept up. Landscaping, a little architectural flair here and there, color schemes, molding, attention to detail, all of this was proof that Habitat houses were built to be homes not just shelters. Millard called it "love in the mortar joints," and it showed.

On East 6th Street on the Lower East Side of Manhattan, we renovated a classic old six-story apartment house, perhaps from the 1920's. Next door the government built a half city-block of low income housing. The Habitat project looks like a classic, 1920's apartment house. The government project looks like a prison, all massive cement and tiny windows. I know they meant well, but ...

A lot of my favorite HFH experiences were demolition derbies. Especially in the early days a Habitat project got off the ground by being given or purchasing at rock bottom prices some dilapidated building. This meant old triple-deckers in Worcester and New Haven, row houses in Baltimore, a huge apartment building in Jersey City, ancient slave quarters in Immokalee, Florida, even an old house given to us if we would move it. Despite years of Habitat construction, I still preferred the fun of *de*construction, so these camps were perfect for me. With our energetic church youth groups, we would go in with crowbars and sledge hammers, filling dumpsters with debris, providing a tangible sense of accomplishment by day's end. We prepared the way for finer work done by finer hands, but we were quite sure that we had the most fun.

We did this for several years at New York City's first HFH project. Our very first workcamp was surreal, a great group of suburban Massachusetts teens on a mid-winter school break, dropped into the middle of a war zone. No exaggeration. Buildings that looked bombed out. Empty lots. Rubble. Everything looking like a skeleton of something that once was, including the people.

I think of the miracle in which Jesus heals a blind man in two stages. After Jesus' first touch, the man said, "I see people, but they look like trees walking." That wasn't good enough for Jesus. He wanted us to see people as people, as real, full of love and potential and dreams, capable of greatness and goodness. So Jesus touched the man again, the famous "second touch."

Habitat was like that. Habitat looked at the Lower East Side, with all its crime and drugs and broken lives and war zone feel, and Habitat saw people as people, full of love and potential and dreams, capable of greatness and goodness.

Not everyone agreed. But we did. My youth group teens were the first volunteers to touch that six-story wreckage of a building. The stairs were long gone, so we had to climb an outdoor fire-escape barely attached to the building, most of the bolts missing. And it was all ours. Our job was to knock down, tear apart, break up, scrape, destroy, and shovel it all down a chute into dumpsters. It should be illegal to have so much fun. It probably was.

For lunch I drove to the nearest McDonald's to buy enough for my hungry team. On the way back my out-of-state license plates caught the suspicious eyes of the police. The Lower East Side was then a notorious drug haven, attracting suburbanites. The Mayor had ordered the neighborhood cordoned off, cops on the corners looking for drug buys. I fit the profile.

"What's in the trunk?" the police asked. "Chicken McNuggets," I declared. They didn't laugh. Believe me, they searched every little box of McNuggets, every little bag of fries.

"What are you doing here?" they then demanded to know. When I told them they were even more suspicious, and escorted me back to the building. They watched our kids climbing the loose fire-escape, swinging sledgehammers, deconstructing in a cloud of dust.

"You should be arrested for child abuse." That was the last word of the day from the police.

But we weren't, and we went back year after year. My partner in this holy lunacy was Paul Davis. We were pastors in neighboring towns before he and his wife, Julie Peeples, left for Americus to become Habitat's Chaplains. For those few years, however, we were just two adult chaperones on a trip far more magical than Disneyland's Magic Kingdom. And *our* place was real.

In my earliest days with Habitat, most people just thought we were crazy, or naïve, or had our heads in the clouds. I was asked if we were a cult, or communist. That actually bothered me. Why would people who were trying to help other people by their own volunteer labor make somebody think of communism? Why wouldn't the first assumption be that we were Christian?

Some did make that assumption.

One winter school break we ended up breaking apart an even bigger apartment house in New Jersey. For a snack break I found a local corner store and bought up all their junk food and soda. As I left, another customer said, "You must be Christians. Because the only people who ever come here to help are either crazy or Christian." Almost the same thing I was told in the mountains of Nicaragua!

Working with Habitat really was a "rush," a natural high. We were looking at the world as Jesus looked at that blind man, willing to give a second touch, even more if necessary, in order to make the world whole. Or at least some little corner of it, or a block or a neighborhood. It was that focus on the local, on the individual, that kept HFH real. In my speeches, I often talked about our work as one house at a time, one family at a time, one brick at a time.

I learned that lesson from my first foray into the world of mission when my focus was on world hunger. Famine in Africa had caught my attention, and I turned some personal African experiences into a personal cause. People were interested but skeptical. When they heard about millions of people starving and millions dying it was too much, too big. The sheer size of the problem discouraged response. It paralyzed people.

As I've mentioned before, my sister and her husband served with HFH in Zaire, now renamed the Congo. In their tiny, remote village there was a woman going blind. Italian Catholic nuns in the area were convinced that an operation in Italy could save her sight, so Donna and David began raising funds. A common response was, "Do you know how many blind people there are in the world!?!" Donna's answer was, "There's only one in this little village, and we can help."

Visiting local HFH projects kept reminding me of the one we can help, instead of being depressed by the ones beyond us. Besides, we figured it was only a matter of time until we got to them, too. Walter Brennan, as an old cowboy, once said, "No brag, just fact." We believed that about ourselves, the hunger for decent housing was ours to satisfy. And we planned to get to everybody. That's why I was so often on the road.

One year I was invited to be the speaker at a traditional Good Friday ecumenical breakfast in Indiana, Pennsylvania. Years later I can recall the sermon easily because I went on to preach the concept many times. *God is a Verb* was the title and concept. God is in the doing, in the loving, in the being. I wasn't trying to create a radical theology, but I was trying to move people away from thinking about God as a passive object out there somewhere awaiting our worship. God is active, God is a doer, God shows initiative, and God takes action. I was taught in P.S. 90 in Queens that the verb carries the action. So does God. From Christmas to the Cross to Easter, God carries the action.

As we choose to emulate God, "to put on Christ," to be "imitators of Christ," to be Godly, to be Christlike, we need to be verb-like. Habitat's enormous success is due in large part to giving lots of people a chance to be verbs. People who would never dare sing in the choir, who would be too intimidated to teach Sunday School, who are too wary or embarrassed to come to Bible Study, who would not think to evangelize or become a missionary, those people and many others are excited to show up at a work site proudly carrying their own tool belt, ready to pour foundations and raise roofs and install plumbing and befriend the neighbors. Love in action. Verbs. Godly. In another book I called it *Nike Theology*. Just do it.

Meeting such people everywhere I went installed a lasting optimism in me about America. A good foundation to face the challenges of today. Nowadays it is popular in the talk show world to harshly criticize other Americans. People are called socialist, communist, fascist, greedy, selfish, lazy, un-American, etc. Our schools stink, we are told, teachers are bad, colleges are full of liberal elites, unions are no good, corporations and newspapers and Hollywood are all leading

America to ruin. By the time you add up all the haters and their hates, there's not much hope for America.

Such thinking never would have built Habitat.

So I'm glad for a lot of years with Habitat people. As I wrote earlier, Habitat is good people doing good things with other good people. That is the real world. The jaded, cynical, hostile, divisive world of the hateful is not everyday America. When I put my Habitat years and my church years together, my life has been immersed in a broad-based America of doing, loving, and compassion. In the months leading up to this book I was stunned by attacks among political pundits on such good words as "social activism" and "empathy." I expect "motherhood" and "apple pie" to be under attack next. Social activism and empathy are at the heart of the American church and the American people. Habitat took those words to the most practical level. Get active in society to such a degree that your pity becomes empathy. That's what happens when you go to a street you don't usually go to, meet folks you don't usually run into, get your lunch at the corner store, play with the neighborhood kids, and work alongside the Habitat family and hear their story.

One Sunday not long ago our church hosted a family which had recently received a Habitat house in Bridgeport, Connecticut. The father looked out at our congregation and smiled, saying, "I recognize some of you. I pave driveways, so I have been to your homes. Never did I know that the people in these homes were building a house for me and my family. While I paved your driveway, you did this for me."

That is one tiny example among a thirty year string of examples that helped immerse our neighborhood into a nearby neighborhood. Over time, neither is the "other." You start to get the feeling that St. Paul knew what he was talking about when he dared to say, "We are one in Christ."

One Last Story

Cazenovia, New York.

I never expected my Habitat days to take me back to Cazenovia. Cazenovia is a little town not far from my college hangout, Colgate University. And I did not fill my Colgate days with glory. My sermons often allude to my failures at college, leading to their very reasonable decision to kick me out. Church members are always pressing me for more detail but I think I'll keep my confession between me and God. Let's just agree that I did way too much of what I wasn't supposed to do, and didn't do much of what I was supposed to do.

Let me go off on a tangent before returning to Cazenovia. A couple of years ago, my wife Alida and I were invited by the Chaplains' Department to come up and give a few presentations to Colgate students interested in religion, Bible, God, the ministry, the sort of thing I gave no attention to when I was there. Alida called it "The David Rowe Redemption Tour."

I was there to proclaim a God I had ignored, to affirm scriptures I had not followed, to promote a faith-based social activism I had not participated in, to partner with a chaplaincy I had nothing to do with, to teach a Gospel I had once forgotten, to advocate a sobriety I had not practiced, to present a Jesus that I had kept at arm's length.

And to give them a little example of what God can do with the wreckage of a dissolute life.

Nothing was more representative of my wasted years than my fraternity life. Driving into Colgate's hometown of Hamilton, New York, we drove to my old fraternity house.

Padlocked. Empty. Over. The cumulative sins of too many guys like me finally caught up to them.

Now, back to Cazenovia.

Our fraternity cook, a woman we greatly mistreated, I'm sure, was from Cazenovia. Cazenovia was the scene of much of my debauchery, either as a destination or on the way to every other destination. I couldn't imagine it was a town that ever cared to see me again.

Imagine my chagrin to be invited, as president of Habitat, to go to Cazenovia as the keynote speaker for the dedication of their first house. I had been in Syracuse for Habitat meetings, the other main locus of my wasted college years. Being in Syracuse as a visiting HFH dignitary was tough enough, but Syracuse is a big city. I could convince myself that my sins in Syracuse were anonymous.

But not in Cazenovia. The first person to greet me, my host for the afternoon, a key part of Cazenovia Habitat, was, of course, my fraternity house cook. She was very gracious, kind, forgiving, and bemused. She wasn't surprised by redemption.

I always use self-deprecating humor or stories in speeches and sermons, so I kicked off my house dedication speech with a 1967 story about getting arrested in Cazenovia. The judge assessed me a huge fine which I couldn't afford, so I asked, "or what?" The Judge said, "thirty days." I said, "I'll take it." The judge softened, and agreed to take something of value until I could pay the fine. I surrendered my baseball glove.

Oh my, the nice folks in Cazenovia loved that story. Later, the man sitting in the front row came up to thank me. Yes, of course, the Judge.

Believe it or not, this visit to Cazenovia wasn't about me. It was about a house, the good neighbors who built the house, and the family about to live in the house.

They were a refugee family, escaped from the killing fields of the Vietnam War and its side effects in neighboring countries. When construction was scheduled to start on their house some of the equipment needed to dig the foundation had not yet arrived. No problem. The family, adults and kids alike, grabbed kitchen utensils, pots, pans, dishes, and started digging. The American Dream isn't for dreamers; it's for doers, workers, diggers. So they dug.

One little story from one little town in one little Habitat project.

I guess that was the first stop on The David Rowe Redemption Tour. It only took me another twenty years to actually make it back to Colgate to finish the job.

Redemption has often been at the heart of Habitat. Rebuilding long ignored neighborhoods, restoring old dilapidated buildings, renewing faith in the lives of volunteers and homeowners. All forms of redemption.

The first HFH worker I ever met was fresh out of prison, working alongside Millard. In the early days of HFH in New York City there was a well-known white collar criminal who escaped prison time by giving his skills and time to Habitat. And after all these years, no one could count all the "community service hours" fulfilled at HFH work sites. All forms of redemption.

Banks and unions, Jimmy Carter and Newt Gingrich, each improved their "street credibility" with some good Habitat work. All forms of redemption.

And me with this little book. A little redemption. A little way to say maybe it was all worth it. It was a long time coming.

Chapter Ten
The End

The very day I sat writing this chapter, my local newspaper carried the story of a group of alleged Christians who came from Texas to visit our nearby town, Bridgeport. They came to stage a protest outside a local Mosque, harassing families of worshippers gathering for Friday prayers. They yelled at Muslim children, and held signs somehow linking Islam, abortion and homosexuality. The newspaper photo accompanying the article showed the Christian ringleader with a t-shirt proclaiming "Jesus is The Standard."

Of what?

Habitat has stood at the cutting edge of Christianity to provide a noble answer, not a narrow answer. Jesus, himself, dared us to be measured by our willingness and our ability to do what is needed "for the least of these." Then Jesus gave some specific examples that begged for a practical solution: the hungry, the thirsty, the lonely, and the imprisoned. That's a "for instance" list: *for instance* feed the hungry, *for instance* clothe the naked. Our job is to look at our world and our time and come up with a current "for instance" list.

That's what Millard did. He took Jesus' very powerful demand, "do unto the least of these as you would do unto me," and added a very logical "for instance . . . those living in a shack, a mud hut, a tenement, a box, or under a bridge."

This was a God-given idea. What Millard's hero out at Koinonia, Clarence Jordan, called "God-breathed." Even for those of us who turned out to be Millard's flotsam and jetsam, even at our worst moments of anger or frustration or hurt, we never doubted that God called Millard to this work, and that he grabbed the call with gusto.

Millard then took the best of evangelical Christianity, and the best of American values, and the best of "the Protestant work ethic," and the best of his own business experience, and created Habitat. Some of us had the privilege to fine tune it, many worked hard to keep it on track, too many suffered when it went awry, and many have helped to restore it.

Perhaps my story adds a useful sentence or two to what is the great story of HFH. If Habitat is great today it is because it had a great beginning with great people, and a great Millard. Those were good days. In the opening chapter I wrote that I believe it is a story worth telling. If you have read this far, you can judge if it was a story worth reading.

I began this book in a convalescent home. In early January, 2010, I had both knees replaced and spent two weeks undergoing physical rehabilitation in a convalescent home. My pen flowed easily, filling pages and filling time. A few weeks later, back home, I began to review those pages. Clearly my pain meds worked well, everything I wrote was bright and cheery. Mind-altered and pain-relieved, I was evidently at last ready to write my Habitat story. Percocet set me free from pain in more ways than one. Of course, eventually I stopped taking the Percocet. I knew there were parts of the story that I needed to tell my way. Not quite Percocet-happy, but not bitter. Truth is, the days I write about were good days with good people.

For a Christmas gift in 1998, I was given a book entitled *Forgiveness,* with the inscription, "it's about time." It was, but it took me another twelve years to get there.

I had considered adding another chapter to this book, *Lessons Learned,* and I had some good ones. They were mostly organizational and structural and institutional.

I'd rather keep it personal. If there is one Habitat lesson worth learning it goes back to the very beginning. Millard's first book was *Bokotola*. He told me that it was the basis for everything he wanted. He took a piece of land used to separate people, to keep people apart in Mbandaka, Zaire. The way Millard told it, *bokotola* was used to describe a buffer property between the white, expatriate, foreigner section of town and the Zairian/Congolese native population. It was a powerful symbol of so much that bedeviled Africa, and humanity. Millard dared to imagine people daring to live beyond those ancient, ingrained traditions of division. Together with helpers and families they turned the division of *Bokotola* into the reconciliation of *Losanganya,* the name he gave to the first Habitat community.

Habitat brought that promise to thousands of towns and villages and cities around the world, *Losanganya* – reconciliation across racial lines, caste lines, religious and political and economic lines. For a lot of years we did that together, Millard and me. But we never did it with each other.

We turned out to be tougher nuts to crack than the villages, towns, cities, and nations that actually believed what we were selling, and took to heart what we talked and taught and preached. Somewhere between the day a few of us sat with him in a hotel in Atlanta and said to our friend, "Millard, we've got a problem," and the day Millard died, it would have been wonderful for us to have accomplished with each other what we so successfully accomplished with others: *Losanganya.*

My guess is that the same things that kept us unreconciled are the same things that keep Christianity from achieving the greatness Christ meant for it. Ego, pride, fear, turf battles, stubbornness. I once said to Millard, "look at all you have accomplished, imagine what you could do if you stopped this stuff," referring to the behaviors that tore us asunder. No doubt Millard wanted to say the same to me.

But the real story is not Millard or me, our successes or failures. The real story is Habitat For Humanity, and the people who took an impossible idea and made it possible. Those people are the real Habitat Heroes.

Who are they? I start with the homeowners, the poor themselves. They took the biggest step, the biggest gamble. Despite decades and even centuries of good reason to mistrust white people, or Christians, or Americans, or outsiders, or do-gooders, they dared to welcome us, accept us, and work with us. Every poor community we worked in across America or around the world could point to broken promises, failed projects, lost trust, exploitation, racist or divisive practices, and just plain rip-offs. Yet they dared to trust again. The poor welcomed us into their lives in the most profound, total, intimate way.

Then there was the community itself, not just the beneficiaries but the local people. Local politicians, local Rotary Club, village chiefs and tribal elders and community leaders. Habitat, as simple as it is, represents thinking way outside the box. Maybe now, after thirty-five years of success and widespread popularity, HFH is mainstream. But not then, not back in the day. Not back when people couldn't decide whether we were communists, or a cult, or just plain crazy. Nevertheless, one by one communities and neighborhoods took a chance.

I am proud to say that churches turned out to be the backbone for HFH. From day one, churches gave us the money, volunteers, credibility, entrée. Churches and pastors and denominations are notorious for protecting their turf. We don't want anything stealing our members, or their time, or their donations, or competing for credit or loyalty. Yet in every town and city there were churches and pastors who understood Habitat's potential not only for the poor and for the community but also for their church life. I have pastored four churches during my HFH life, and there has been nothing but gain for each church in the relationship. I believe in the concept that "a rising tide lifts all boats," and as churches invested time, money and people in Habitat the return on investment was all positive. Certainly in the churches I have served, the more we gave to HFH in work hours and money, the stronger the church was. When you put together fulfilled volunteers with tangible results with inspiring stories with good press, you end up with a church that feels good about itself – and people do more and give more. All to the good.

My last category of Habitat Heroes is the worker-bees, the unsung heroes behind the scenes who literally put their lives and careers on the line for HFH. At some point, back around 1977 or so, Habitat had to become more than Millard. For that to happen, men and women gave up professions and hometowns and retirements, putting off graduate school, foregoing promotions, risking savings, all in the belief that Habitat was an idea whose time had come. They ended up in Americus and Uganda and Papua New Guinea and Guatemala, and in towns all over the United States, pursuing this disarmingly simple idea articulated by Millard. Namely, that every night, all over the world, people get sleepy. And they ought to be able to go to bed safe and secure, snug in their bed. No dust and mud underneath them, no scorpions or snakes falling from the thatch overhead, no wind whirling through the wall slats, none of the indignity or uncertainty of renting at someone's whim or fancy.

Somebody had to believe that Millard was right. Somebody had to believe that folks could do something about it.

Those somebodies are the worker-bees of Habitat's world, from Saturday morning volunteers showing up at a worksite with a hammer dug out of the kitchen drawer, to the career change professionals who chose a new path for their lives.

My favorite cartoon features three little bird-like characters. Two of them are standing at the edge of a very dangerous cliff, looking sadly at a third figure who has stumbled over the edge, and is barely hanging on for dear life by the tips of his fingers.

"Tsk, tsk, tsk," one mutters solemnly.

The other says, "Somebody oughta do something".

The best story of Habitat is the story of all those somebodies who echoed the prophet Isaiah, "here am I, use me!"

Those somebodies fill my church, Greenfield Hill Congregational Church, people who never say "no" or "can't" or "won't." People motivated by faith who just *do*.

The challenge I made to Millard, to imagine what could be accomplished if we were unshackled from our weaknesses, is a challenge for Christianity. St. Paul wrote a beautiful phrase, "whatsoever is true, noble, right, pure, lovely, admirable, think about such things . . . (and) put it into practice" (Philippians 4:8-9). That is what Habitat can mean for Christianity. Whatsoever Habitat does that is noble, bold, daring, compassionate, faithful, reconciling, helpful, hopeful – bring that into your church life, your faith life. Think about it, and put it into practice. Do it. In this way the best of Habitat just gets better.

Millard's audacious declaration, that we would eliminate substandard housing from the face of the earth and then tackle something else, remains audacious and daring, as bold as the Gospel itself. It is our unfinished business.

A couple of years after Hurricane Katrina devastated so many families, Habitat came under unfair criticism for not doing enough fast enough. In all honesty that was probably the first day I was proud since the day so many of us were fired. I was proud that Habitat had dared to step where the odds were long, the risks were great, the obstacles huge, and the criticism likely.

It didn't matter. As in my good old days, Habitat does the best they can with what they have. As in my good old days, it is still about one house at a time, one brick at a time, one family at a time.

So I now come to the end of my Habitat story, still wondering where I fit in with the Habitat world, the world outside my own memories. Am I the bad guy, infamous, a Northern liberal, 'defender of women,' demonic? Or am I a little part of a larger story that was well worth it all?

It took me fourteen years to live this story, twenty more to get over it and through it and to the point of being glad for being part of it.

Before putting this book to bed, I took one more step forward that, surprisingly, took me way back.

Driving along the old Mohawk Trail in rural western Massachusetts, I saw a Habitat house under construction. I pulled over, and climbed the little front yard hill to where volunteers were hard at work. Late summer, hot August, lunchtime, and they were still at it, and proud to talk about it.

The house was very energy-efficient, it was explained to me, a thorough renovation of an old dilapidated eyesore, a hotbed of activity for two local colleges, and soon to be the pride and joy of a hardworking family. It was talking about the family that really sparked the conversation, more than the house. "They're already past five hundred hours of their own sweat equity poured into this house," the local Habitat guy told me. "And they won't stop until they get one thousand, that's their goal: one thousand hours of their own volunteer work."

Before I left, I asked the volunteer why he did it. "It feels good," he said, with a really nice smile, "it's so much fun. And there's nothing better than the moment when we turn that house over to the family. We give them the keys, we built it together, and now it's their home."

"God bless you for that," I said.

And I meant it.

FOCI, Habitat and Me

Who knows? Maybe this book will even do some good for Habitat. As I wrote at the beginning, someone's "good old days" regarding Habitat are being constructed right now. Millard's vision, and everyone's hard work, paid off like Jesus' Parable of the Sower, one hundred fold. If this book helps connect my Habitat "good old days" with tomorrow's, that's great! Contact Habitat at www.Habitat.org.

But since you have read this far, maybe a little interest will rub off on my little mission, FOCI.

The back story: I went to India in 1983 to scout out the best place to start Habitat's first project in Asia. While I was there, God literally challenged me to start Friends of Christ in India (FOCI). Fortunately, God also teamed me up with Azariah, my Indian partner in mission until his death in 2010. Together we created a mission that touches the poorest of the poor with dignity, integrity, love and peace. Following Azariah's mantra of "see a need, meet a need," we do just that: lots of kids in schools, food for the hungry, care for the elderly, the healing touch of doctors and nurses, fresh water, good churches, signs of hope all around. Try our website: www.FOCI.org.

As for me? Any author writes for an audience, and hopes that the book creates a connection. I'd be honored to hear from you. Send me your thoughts ... or more book orders! I can be reached at:

DRowe@greenfieldhillchurch.com

or Greenfield Hill Church, 1045 Old Academy Road, Fairfield CT 06824